A word about this series from **Toastmasters International . . .**

Who needs another book on public speaking, let alone a series of them? After all, this is a skill best learned by practice and "just doing it," you say.

True, but insight from people who've already been where you are might help ease some bumps along the road and provide handy advice on handling stagefright and knotty speech assignments.

After all, if practice is the best solution to public speaking excellence, why is this country so full of speakers who can't speak effectively? Consider politicians, business executives, sales professionals, teachers, and clerics who often fail to reach their audience because they make elementary mistakes, such as speaking too fast or too long, failing to prepare adequately, and forgetting to analyze their audiences.

Too often, we assume that because we try so hard to communicate, people will automatically understand us. Nothing could be further from the truth! Listeners will judge us by what they think we said, rather than what was intended or even said. Simply put, the meaning of our message—and our credibility—is determined by the reaction we get from other people. The purpose of *The Essence of Public Speaking Series,* then, is to help you in the communication process, prepare you for the unexpected, warn you of the pitfalls, and, as a result, ensure that the message you want to give is indeed the same one people hear.

This series represents the accumulated wisdom of experts in various speech-related fields. The books are written by academically trained professionals who have spent decades writing and delivering speeches, as well as training others. The series covers the spectrum of speaking scenarios: writing for the ear, using storytelling and humor, customizing particular topics for various audiences, motivating people to action, using technology for presentations, and other important topics.

Whether you are an inexperienced or seasoned public speaker, *The Essence of Public Speaking Series* belongs on your bookshelf. Because no matter how good you are, there is always room for improvement. The key to becoming a more effective speaker is in your hands: Do you have the self-discipline to put into practice the techniques and advice outlined in these books?

I honestly believe that every person who truly wants to become a confident and eloquent public speaker can become one. Success or failure in this area solely depends on attitude. There is no such thing as a "hopeless case." So, if you want to enhance your personal and professional progress, I urge you to become a better public speaker by doing two things:

- Read these books.
- Get on your feet and practice what you've learned.

Terrence J. McCann
Executive Director, Toastmasters International

. . . and from the National Speakers Association

For the true professional, school is never out. *The Essence of Public Speaking Series* was developed to share ideas and information with those who desire to accelerate their development as speakers. As a community of more than 3,700 men and women dedicated to advancing the art and value of experts who speak professionally, the National Speakers Association (NSA) welcomes this comprehensive educational resource.

A broad spectrum of talented individuals make up the field of professional speaking: consultants, trainers, educators, humorists, industry specialists, authors, and many more. NSA brings this wide variety of professional speakers together to better serve their clients, advance their careers, and help them reach a higher level of personal and professional development.

Throughout *The Essence of Public Speaking Series,* you will hear the voices of NSA members offering their expertise and experiences. This sharing of ideas and knowledge is a key element of NSA membership. NSA's founder and Chairperson Emeritus Cavett Robert said, "Experience is the only thing that's worth more secondhand than first-hand. We don't live long enough to learn through trial and error, so it's best to get your O.P.E. degree—Other People's Experience."

The "information age" is creating a huge demand for professional speakers. The fact that education is one of the top growth industries in the world should come as no surprise. What may seem surprising, however, is the fact that when we're speaking of education, we are not referring to the traditional colleges and universities. Instead, it is the learning that is conducted daily in the hotels and corporate training facilities. The "faculty" for these learning experiences are often professional speakers.

Speakers are a key element in the growing meetings business. The American Society of Association Executives reports that the meeting market is a $75 billion industry. Moreover, the American Society for Training and Development estimates that well over $100 billion is expended annually in the field of human resource development alone.

The audiences of the new millennium will be different from the audiences of the past. They are not content to sit and be passive listeners; they want to take an active role in their own learning; and require cutting-edge information presented in a technologically savvy manner. The speakers and trainers who fail to deliver the information and content these audiences can utilize immediately will notice that audiences are not afraid to vote with their feet.

So, we welcome you to the world of speaking. As you read the volumes in this series, you will explore many facets of public and professional speaking. You are about to embark on an important learning experience—one that will broaden your vision as a public speaker and perhaps instill a desire to make speaking an important dimension of your career. NSA, the "Voice of the Speaking Profession," stands ready to provide you with information on the speaking industry and the resources you need to make a speaking career a viable option.

Edward E. Scannell, CSP, CMP
Interim Executive Vice President
National Speakers Association

"If you want to skyrocket your career as a platform professional, this is your guide to absolute success. A practical, step-by-step plan for marketing yourself—and for creating your own powerful niche in the world of speaking."

— Glenna Salsbury, CSP, CPAE, Professional Speaker and author of *The Art of The Fresh Start*

"The profession of speaking is growing astronomically. This great book by Bill Thompson has all the step by step how-to instructions. Bill Thompson knows exactly how the game works for those who are serious about the world of paid speaking. We enthusiastically endorse this book."

— Dottie Walters, President, Walters International Speakers Bureau, Publisher *Sharing Ideas Magazine for Speakers,* Author *Speak & Grow Rich,* Prentice Hall.

"This is a terrific book. It is substantive, interesting, and very practical. Read it to learn new strategies, chart new courses, and uncover new opportunities."

— Nido R. Qubein, Chair, Creative Services, Inc., National Speakers Association member and honor recipient

"Thanks to the author, there is a comprehensive, concise, and clear overview of the speaking industry. Speaking for Profit and Pleasure *is an essential foundation for the would-be professional speaker and a beneficial refresher for the person who is already making money by speaking. It mirrors its own name by being both pleasurable and profitable to read."*

— Dana LaMon, Toastmasters International Accredited Speaker, 1992 World Champion of Public Speaking, and author

"After speaking more than ten years 'for profit and pleasure' I can truly say that Mr. Thompson certainly knows what he is talking about. [This book] gives great

insight, plenty of details and 'how tos' as well as warnings of possible pitfalls. He covers the subject of public speaking thoroughly! I truly enjoyed the information from beginning to end, and would highly recommend his material to anyone considering this field."

— Pauline Harvey, DTM, Certified Local Pastor, Toastmasters International Accredited Speaker

"Speaking for Profit and Pleasure *is an excellent resource for demonstrating to students how they can convert the speaking skills they learn in the classroom into success outside the classroom. Perhaps the greatest interest to today's students, this text offers an insightful analysis of the growing area of avocational (part-time professional) speaking. It also does a wonderful job of explaining step-by-step how individuals can turn their public speaking skills into a successful business, and it offers numerous professional profiles of individuals whose presentational skills have led to professional success. In short, this text offers an abounding answer to the perpetual student query, what can I really do with public speaking?"*

— David G. Levasseur, Ph.D., Communication Studies Dept., West Chester University of Pennsylvania, Select Toastmaster member

"Speaking for Profit and Pleasure *is a systematic and well-structured approach to the business side of speaking. Among other things, it provides a unique and excellent compendium of the principles and opportunities for avocational speaking on the public platform. It will serve a growing market for the services of those who choose to speak part-time, in addition to pursuing their traditional occupations."*

— Dr. Edwin A. Hollatz, Professor of Speech Communication, Wheaton College, Wheaton, IL

SPEAKING FOR PROFIT AND PLEASURE

Making the Platform Work for You

WILLIAM D. THOMPSON

ALLYN AND BACON

Boston London Toronto Sydney Tokyo Singapore

A Viacom Company
160 Gould Street
Needham Heights, MA 02194

Internet: www.abacon.com
America Online: keyword: College Online

ISBN 0-205-27026-3

Printed in the United States of America
10 9 8 7 6 5 4 3 2 1   02 01 00 99 98 97

Contents

Foreword

In spite of this book's relatively objective style, I want to make clear at the outset that this book has come straight out of my life.

My first full-time job in my early 20s was teaching college speech courses. With a Ph.D. from Northwestern University in speech communication I began a career in university and theological seminary classrooms and, for one year, taught an interesting group of students at England's Cambridge University (while Prince Charles was studying there—my only real claim to fame!). Most of those years I was writing and delivering sermons nearly every week as a bivocational minister, utilizing the divinity degree I had also earned. For 12 years, I trained several hundred U.S. Army and U.S. Navy chaplains from all faith traditions in four-day advanced preaching workshops on three continents.

After moving from academia into the business world, my sermons metamorphosed into motivational speeches and the college lectures into presentation skills training sessions for business executives, some whom I wrote speeches for and others whom I coached. In my spare time, I started and managed a speakers bureau that for eight years furnished free speakers to community groups and provided paid speakers for corporations and associations. Through that bureau, I experienced the speaking business vicariously through working with hundreds of speakers, paid and unpaid. I found support and growth through membership in the National Speakers Association, the International Group of Agencies and Bureaus, and the American Society for Training and Development. I recently discovered the value of keeping my skills sharp at a Toastmasters club, where I became a Competent Toastmaster, held office as vice president of education, and took home some "best speaker" ribbons.

I have written books on speaking and listening, helped to start and nurture the Academy of Homiletics and the Religious Speech Communication Association, and offered help to some wonderful people in my public seminars on "Speaking as a Second Income."

You can discern as you read, I hope, that I think it is important for people to get up in front of a group to tell what they know, say what they believe, and, above all, communicate something of themselves. It's the way to change the world!

William D. Thompson

Preface

Why would you—or anyone—open a book on public speaking? If it is to learn how to prepare and present a speech, you will be disappointed with this one. It serves a very different purpose. Its purpose is to put public speaking in perspective for people who want to enrich their lives and livelihoods through public speaking.

Since the world began, people have been speaking in public. Long before Corax and Tisias set up the first school for speakers in the fifth century B.C.E., people who wanted to share what they knew, to make people laugh, or to get people to change their minds were standing up and talking to groups of people.

Along with the rest of civilized life at the turn of this millennium, the study of public speaking has become quite sophisticated. A great deal of help is available for people who wish to do it well—books, tapes, coaching, courses, seminars—providing in considerable detail the principles and techniques of this significant dimension of human communication.

What is less well understood is the role of public speaking in society and especially in business—who does it, for what reasons, and with what results. This book takes the reader behind and beyond the two or three pages in the standard speech textbook that are titled something like "The Importance of Public Speaking in Society" to a real-time look at the world of corporate trainers, Toastmasters, CEOs speaking at shareholder meetings, humorists at the convention's final banquet, motivational speakers at sales rallies, lecturers on the college circuit, returned travelers at their Rotary Club luncheons, financial planners at seminars for clients and prospects, politicians seeking votes or support for their bills and . . . well, where does the list end? This book attempts to answer in some detail the question, Why should I devote my time and energy to a public speaking course, or to membership in a Toastmasters club, or even to reading a book on public speaking?

The *pleasure* of it, for one thing. Many people speak simply because of the pleasure they receive speaking to audiences who enjoy hearing them and of doing something to change their world. Others speak to earn monetary *profit,* sometimes a great deal of it. But both the profit and the process of earning it are undoubtedly a source of considerable pleasure for those who make money in the process. So even the simple distinction in this book's title, *Speaking for Profit and Pleasure,* requires some exploration for people who are wondering just how public speaking, one of humankind's oldest activities, fits into their lives.

We will look first at the *why* of public speaking, but not in the standard categories that describe the purposes of a single speech—to inform, motivate, entertain, or persuade. We will try rather to describe the values that people derive from participating in the activity called public speaking. And we will go beyond the why—the values to the speaker, the community, and the speaker's vocation—to provide practical, step-by-step help for those who are exploring the *how* of putting public speaking skills to work in order to achieve financial reward.

Part I of the book will be of value to everyone who is taking a serious interest in public speaking, whether for personal development, for service to the community, or for achieving excellence in a job.

Part II, one chapter, will explore the world of learning to speak and helping others to speak well. It should become apparent that a commitment to growing will earn tremendous rewards, whether you are learning or teaching, or doing both.

Part III will investigate the commercial world of speaking. It will interest persons who believe that what they have to say may contribute to their income, directly or indirectly, and these chapters will provide abundant, detailed, and practical help for developing that income. Indeed, the chapters on avocational speaking and full-time professional speaking constitute a detailed manual on how to be successful in developing income as a speaker.

The final chapter takes a bird's eye view of the industry that has developed around the world of public speaking. It provides the hitherto untold story of the people and organizations that owe their livelihood to public speakers—who supply their needs for instruction, consultation, goods and equipment, marketing support, and association with each other.

The appendix provides eight lists of useful resources and six sample documents to facilitate the reader's pusuit of public speaking—for pleasure or for profit.

This book will have achieved one of its most important goals if you read something that makes you say, "Aha, that's something I can do . . . I can use that skill in my work . . . I can speak on that subject . . . I can see where I might find fulfillment in the speaking business . . . I can see the value of that course I am taking . . . I can see how all the elements fit together . . . I believe I can make a difference." That's the aim—to make a difference, in your life and in your world.

ACKNOWLEDGMENTS

Whatever is of value in this book is here because (1) a long time ago, Dr. Clarence L. Nystrom invited me to teach public speaking at Wheaton College in Illinois while I was still in graduate school, launching me on a career in public speaking; (2) a great many college and graduate students, business leaders, and military officers taught me at least as much as I taught them; (3) Dottie Walters introduced me to the world of professional speaking and fed me through stimulating conversations, books, and tapes; (4) the Liberty Bell Chapter of the National Speakers Association enriched me with learning and leadership opportunities; and (5) the Select Toastmasters club of Media, Pennsylvania, provided friendship and encouragement in my continuing journey to become an effective speaker.

A Responsible Society

THE RIGHT TO SPEAK

If you are a citizen of the United States, you are a citizen of a free land where you are guaranteed by the Constitution the right to speak your mind freely. That right extends to your neighbors and coworkers, giving them the opportunity to express whatever attitudes and opinions they believe are important to their community and to themselves.

Unlike a totalitarian state, where people live by the judgments of rulers who have seized power, our country gives its citizens the right to introduce and debate the issues that define the quality of its life. From an individual citizen speaking at a school board meeting to a U.S. senator speaking to a full Senate chamber, every citizen enjoys the right to be heard.

It is the rare speech that, by itself, changes a long-held policy, much less the course of a nation. What that means is that a free nation's citizens must be everlastingly at the process of public speaking. Minds work cautiously—as they should—while people investigate the adequacy of the speaker's data and reasoning. Decisions come gradually as listeners explore various alternatives to the ideas being presented and the consequences of each.

As ideal as this system is, it does not always work well. Throughout our history, African Americans, Native Americans, and many Asian Americans have been denied the right to speak as they believe and to live where they wish. Today, increasing numbers of Hispanic Americans are still struggling to be heard. While some of America's finest speaking has been done by women, only within the lifetimes of many persons still living have they been given the right to express their opinions by casting their ballots at the polls. As the wealth of individuals and special interest organizations increases, they may exercise disproportionate influence on public policy by dominating the channels of communication and decision making. The right to run for public office is severely inhibited by the high cost of campaigning, especially the high cost of television time.

The freedom of speech ideal is as strong as ever—perhaps stronger than ever. Opportunities abound in every community to speak and be heard. Civic organizations meet in nearly every community—to achieve safer streets, improved lighting, more efficiently run local government, modernized transportation, and a healthier environment. Trade associations work to get more favorable treatment from government regulators. Members of churches, synagogues, and mosques rise in congregational and denominational meetings to ask questions and propose new actions. Parents confront school boards and administrators with demands for higher quality education. Public access cable television channels are everywhere, made available by law, for members of the community to be heard.

THE OPPORTUNITIES TO SPEAK

How many people find themselves in front of an audience on any given day? The numbers are staggering. Who are these people and why are they speaking? The variety is astounding and the reasons almost as varied as the people.

If you could simultaneously look into every meeting room in your community on one day of the week where one person is talking to a group of people, you would be astonished at the sheer number of speakers. You might start with the school classrooms—from kindergarten to a graduate seminar at the nearest university. Move then to the courthouse, where lawyers are presenting cases to juries. Stop for a moment at the hospital to overhear a physician addressing a staff meeting. Down the hallway, a human relations consultant talks to health care aides about teamwork. In a restaurant meeting room on the other side of town, a representative of an HMO urges a small group of Medicare recipients to sign up for a Medigap policy for no monthly premiums. At the community college, students are lining up to buy tickets for a talk by a nominated U.S. cabinet officer who was forced to withdraw because of an episode of political incorrectness. A group of accountants is taking a coffee break during a daylong seminar mandated by the state to meet its annual requirements for continuing education hours.

Across town, a Rotary Club is applauding a visiting volunteer speaker from the local Red Cross unit who encouraged the members to show up at the nearby fire station the following day to make a blood donation. In a hotel meeting room out on the highway, several dozen women gather at a public seminar on assertiveness in the workplace sponsored by Career Track, a public seminar company. A minister speaks to an inspirational noontime gathering of people on their lunch hours in the chapel of her church. Twenty-one employees of the electric utility gather for an after-hours meeting of their corporate Toastmasters club, where they will present impromptu Table Topics and hear several of their fellow employees deliver prepared talks. A candidate for Congress clarifies his stand on Social Security and Medicare to a senior citizen group meeting in the community center. A union leader explains to his blue-collar listeners the reasons for and against accepting their company's proposed work-rule changes.

In a very important sense, public speaking is the lubricant that makes the gears of society run smoothly.

Who gives these speeches in your area? A recent study in a region including three small cities—Albany-Schenectady-Troy (New York)—indicated that, of a sample of about 500 adults, between 55 and 63 percent of them gave at least one speech in the preceding 2 years to 10 or more people. Almost three quarters of them gave at least four speeches—mostly job-related. As might be expected, the better-educated, higher-income people gave the most presentations. Speech making, it would seem, is far more common and widespread than most people think.

The group responsible for the most speeches given in any year is easily Toastmasters International. Since its founding in the 1920s, an ever-increasing number of Toastmasters clubs have been forming to provide the opportunity for the development of speaking and leadership skills. With more than 8,000 clubs meeting weekly in groups of 20 to 30 people, the sheer number of speeches given is astonishing. If each club hears 3 speeches during each meeting, Toastmasters is responsible for 24,000 speeches a week. If the average number of club meetings in a year is 40, about 1 million prepared Toastmasters speeches are given every year, and that doesn't count the more numerous two-minute impromptu speeches that would more than double or even triple that figure!

At the national level, meetings involving speakers have become one of the largest industries in the United States. Trade associations, individual membership societies, and voluntary organizations that make up the American Society of Association Executives (ASAE)

> dominate the $83 billion meetings industry, spending more than $56 billion annually to hold conventions, expositions and seminars. The entire meetings industry ranks as the 23rd largest contributor to the Gross National Product. ASAE members collectively planned

> 375,980 meetings, expositions and seminars in 1993–1994, involving 272,146,200 delegates.[1]

Practically all these meetings are addressed by speakers, paid or unpaid. In a recent 3-year period, conventions and annual meetings increased 11 percent and educational seminars increased 19 percent. Every informed prediction projects increasing growth. Also increasing is the number of meetings outside the United States.

A significant number of those speakers have formed their own trade group, the National Speakers Association (NSA), currently numbering about 3,700. Each member is a professional speaker, having spoken at least 10 times for a fee. Members meet annually in national and regional gatherings and monthly in 37 local and state chapters. The National Association of Campus Activities (NACA) brings speakers and college audiences together in 11 regional conferences and a national convention, where speakers compete for time to showcase their presentations geared to college audiences.

Speakers are even hired by cruise companies to entertain and inform vacationers. One cruise line recently hired speakers on such topics as the Civil War, golf, gardening, wine, photography, and computers. Many business gatherings take place on cruise ships, where speakers address such topics as sales techniques, the global economy, and leadership.

In many communities of modest size, local speakers earn from $50 to $500 for a single talk or training session. More than half the groups that pay speakers for business or association convention addresses use at least two speakers, paying each a median fee of $2,000. Speakers at educational seminars receive somewhat less, earning a median fee of $800. Speakers who work for public seminar companies such as Career Track, Fred Pryor, and SkillPath earn $200 to $500 a day plus commissions on books and tapes they sell. If you can see yourself taking a place in the speaking industry, you may find these categories and fee ranges to represent an attractive option.

THE SPEAKER AS A PERSON

While speakers exert a powerful influence on society, not just any kind of speaker will make ours a better world. Even a beautifully polished presentation by a company president may sour the workforce on the company's viability if the employees do not trust their president. The masterful speech of a dictator like Hitler or Stalin may provoke the slaughter of innocent people if the speaker reinforces the dark side of the audience's nature. The specious arguments of a citizen before a civic group may achieve change, but the community may suffer irreparable harm from that change.

Speaking responsibly requires a great deal more than the technical skills that can be mastered by almost anyone—research, organization, language, and delivery skills. Quintilian, teaching in Rome in the first century, taught that the model public speaker is "a good person speaking well." The effective speaker not only should be a good person but also should "above all things devote . . . attention to the formation of moral character and must acquire a complete knowledge of all that is just and honorable."[2]

Centuries before Quintilian's time, Aristotle told his students in Athens that speaking responsibly and effectively requires three elements; he called them the means of persuasion. The speaker, he taught, must be able to provide the listeners with reliable information, carefully organized so that they can understand and evaluate its importance. He called this element *logos*. He taught also that the speaker must be able to move an audience emotionally, using a quality he named *pathos*. To engage the feelings of the audience involves using narrative skillfully and employing language that is colorful, graphic, and sensory. He called for metaphors to arouse images in peoples' minds. But he lifted to the greatest importance a quality he called *ethos,* the prime means of persuasion. In today's culture, it would be roughly translated as *credibility. Ethos,* he wrote, consists of competence, integrity, and goodwill. Audiences don't necessarily distinguish among these elements, as some recent research has discovered, but they have guided speakers to excellence for several millennia.

Competence

Competence is a factor in the speaking equation that refers to the speaker's knowledge of the subject. That knowledge comes from personal experience, research, or both. While it is sometimes possible for a clever person to fool an audience, most audiences can detect incompetence from the materials that don't quite fit or the subtle clues the speaker's voice or body gives away. If the speech itself doesn't reveal the speaker's incompetence, the question-and-answer session may.

Becoming a competent speaker involves working hard at exploring and arranging one's own experience with a subject. For some speaking situations, you will dig deeply into your store of knowledge gleaned from research you have done, travel you have taken, family crises you have weathered, business challenges you have overcome, experiments you have succeeded in making work—or seen fail. Audiences respond favorably to someone who has "been there, done that."

The competent speaker also draws on the experience of others. Beginning speakers may start by lamely quoting Webster's dictionary to define a term or by rearranging material from the *Reader's Digest,* but they quickly reveal the shallowness of their preparation. With a universe of information available through an extraordinary number of books, periodicals, and tapes for sale and in libraries—and especially now through the Internet—there is no excuse for anyone to give a speech that lacks substance.

Integrity

Integrity may be difficult for an audience to judge because it most accurately defines the speaker's *persona,* and that—as one of my teachers put it—"is better felt than telt." The word *integrity* comes from the same root as the mathematical term *integer,* meaning a whole number. What an audience expects—and deserves—is a speaker who is "a whole number," a person who is put together properly and committed to what is true, right, and just. A rough synonym for *integrity* is *character,* sometimes defined as what you are and do when no one is looking—in contradistinction to *reputation,* what you portray to others. A speaker with integrity will, in the right circumstances, provide a hearing for contrary ideas. A speaker with integrity will demean or embarrass no one. A speaker with integrity will credit sources of the speech's ideas or materials.

Why is integrity so important to an audience? Audiences in our culture possess a set of values that honors right over wrong. In spite of the all-too-pervasive lawlessness that claims the attention of the media, we are basically a law-abiding people who are committed to honesty. We want what is right and good for ourselves, our children, and our institutions. Beyond its commitment to the obvious intrinsic value of integrity, every audience is characterized by a kind of implicit integrity of its own—the integrity that defines its purpose for being. Its members will honor and respond to a speaker with integrity—whose purpose is likewise clear, coherent, and purposeful.

Goodwill

Goodwill is not a commonly used term in English, and it may be totally unfamiliar in the context of public speaking. It means that the speaker's motives are centered on the needs of the audience. When Aristotle used that term, he was distressed by teachers of speech in Athens called sophists, who were urging their students to display their flamboyant style—precisely timed gestures, elaborate sentence construction, stories calculated to evoke laughter and tears. He reminded his students that audiences would inevitably see through such self-serving speech, and that justice—not to speak of the then-new democratic way of life—would not be served by empty, grandiloquent oratory.

Unfortunately, the pressure to cut corners, to use borrowed information without giving credit, to mislead with statistics, and to exaggerate did not end twenty-five hundred years ago, however valid and valuable Aristotle's advice. That pressure is increasing in our society with its accelerated pace and its increasing deficit of ethical and moral standards. Participation in any public speaking event carries with it choices that deserve the most honest decision making the speaker can invoke. Just as you expect high *ethos*—rigorous honesty—from a professor, a counselor, a clergyperson, a journalist, a spouse, a salesperson, or a manager, you and every member of every audience expect and deserve reliable information from a speaker, truthfully conveyed.

The speaker who communicates solid, well-prepared material to an audience demonstrates goodwill in abundance—a concern that the listeners become better informed, more highly motivated people. The speaker's *ethos* rises to the extent that people sense that the speaker's agenda is their good.

NOTES

1. "Associations in a Nutshell," American Society of Association Executives, 1575 I Street, NW, Washington, DC 20005-1168.

2. Reprinted by permission of the publishers and the Loeb Classical Library from Quintilian, *Institutionis Oratoriae,* vol. 12, translated by H. E. Butler, Cambridge, Mass: Harvard University Press, 1961.

2 Personal Development

People who develop public speaking skills may also develop into better human beings. They may take a speech course or join a Toastmasters club to become more productive employees, to learn how to market their professional practice by giving seminars, or to enter the appealing world of paid speaking. However, some wonderful things happen on the road to that goal.

THE JOY OF SHARING

Of the thousands of topics on which people speak, you have one—or a few—you delight to talk about. Chances are that you have been talking about technology, time management, or taxes for a long time; the subject is intimately tied up with your vocation or your values—or both. You now see yourself on a platform, talking about that very topic for the sheer delight of it. Perhaps a fee will come to you—or the commendation of a professor or an audience member—but the fundamental reason you are there is to share with others some ideas and experiences you have found interesting or challenging. Something you say may change another person's life for the better, and that is reason to celebrate.

Altruism, "the unselfish concern for the welfare of others," characterizes one of the finest human traits. Even if the desire to share what you know were a one-time phenomenon, it would make giving a speech a worthwhile activity. But that desire is a powerful motivator that drives each of us to communicate our information or values to ever-increasing numbers of people. Many gifted speakers spend a lifetime speaking to school groups about smoking or drug abuse because they feel so deeply about these subjects.

The best part of speaking from altruistic motives is that the joy of sharing multiplies itself. Especially when audiences respond favorably to your message, you feel deeply rewarded for exercising one of your most important gifts, the generous urge to share, and you gain renewed impetus to keep sharing. Like love, the more you give away, the more you have to give.

THE JOY OF GROWING

Many people who think hopefully about speaking in public give up before they start. They are victims of speech apprehension, commonly known as stage fright. A study published in London, England's *Sunday Times* in 1973 reported that among three thousand Americans the fear of public speaking was greater than the fear of heights, insects and bugs, financial problems, deep water, sickness, death, flying, loneliness, and dogs—in that order. While highly suspect as valid research, the report has been widely published to support the very genuine fear of public speaking that many people possess. The opportunity to take a speech course or participate in a Toastmasters club is the best opportunity they will ever have to overcome the fear of speaking in public. Moving beyond that fear—if you have it—is the first step in the joy of growing.

Preparing a speech is another step in the joy of growing. The conscientious speaker rummages through books or magazines, quizzes knowledgeable people, and searches personal experience to find just the right material for a speech. Browsing the web rewards the genuinely curious with a joy of discovery that previous generations were unable to experience. Many Toastmasters feel that giving a speech on new and different topics every few weeks has stretched their minds and added to their stores of knowledge in ways few other people have experienced.

Except for extremely technical subjects, just about every area of human knowledge is open to investigation and understanding by persons with active, inquiring minds. Even the disciplines of astrophysics, biblical hermeneutics, and neuropsychiatry offer popularized versions of their fields—if you know where to find them—yielding some fascinating insights to those willing to investigate. The explosion of knowledge—the world's store of information doubles every 18 months, it is said—promises an endless supply of data to be absorbed and translated into speech material. An incalculable amount of the world's knowledge is now available through the Internet and through an avalanche of CDs on the shelves of software stores and even supermarkets.

The acquisition of that information, once a relatively simple quest through a library's card file or the discovery of magazine articles through the *Reader's Guide to Periodical Literature,* is now a daunting and challenging task. There is so much information out there, so many leads to be tracked down, and so little time to do it! The aspirant for public speaking skill, in college or on the professional platform, is forced to keep research tools sharpened. Fortunately, the tools of research are self-sharpening as they are used. Each quest yields not only the information but a heightened awareness of what is available and skill in how to find it. The study and practice of public speaking, perhaps more than any other, represents a fight against the intellectual inertia that would keep our minds static. And the adage remains that the best way to learn something is to teach it.

For 22 years, I was in the advertising industry. I owned my own agency, won a lot of awards, built it up to $22 million with 50 employees and 3 offices with affiliations in Australia and London, and I was terrified of speaking. I had been asked to speak at different conferences, and I turned them down. My competitors would take the assignments and get millions of dollars in exposure and business that we lost. Even when I had to present a new campaign to clients, I would bring my sales people and say, "You go ahead and get the experience of speaking." I was looked upon as a mentor, a nurturer. "Isn't she wonderful?" people would say. "She's really fostering the growth of her staff." But it was just my terror. When I closed my business, I started working for someone else, but my husband said, "Come, work with me in Gedaliah Communications: Speaking for Results. I've been doing it alone for nine years. You're a business-woman; run my business."

We went together to a national Toastmasters conference, and I did not want to be there; I had a chip on my shoulder. The night of the international contest, the nine finalists came out on the stage. One of the contestants was one of the worst speakers I had ever heard. When we got back to our room, Robert said, "Here you are, afraid to speak in front of three people, and you have the nerve to talk about someone who's up on the stage in front of two thousand people! These people may not be the best speakers in the world, but they've got the courage to be there! Look around! There's a guy without any legs; he's up there. And there's a guy who's blind. And there's a woman with an accent. And there's someone who stutters. And they're all up on that stage. And you won't speak in front of three people! I'm teaching executives all over the world how to get past their fears, and my own wife, who's working with me, won't learn how to speak—won't even try it!" It was the biggest fight we ever had.

We returned to New York and Robert took me to a Toastmasters meeting. I wouldn't even introduce myself.

But at the end of the meeting, I wrote my check and joined. It was September, and I put off my first speech to the middle of November: and I was dying. I practiced it four thousand times. A week before I was to give it, I lost my voice. No sound. Three days before the meeting, I started throwing up. The day before, the assigned Toastmaster called me to get some information to introduce me. I passed out. Robert found me on the floor with the phone next to me! The afternoon of the meeting was an out-of-body experience. I had practiced so much that the words just came out. I finished the speech, and I couldn't wait to get out of the room. But they voted me best speaker of the day!

It's the best thing that ever happened to me because it's given me a career. And now, when I teach people how to communicate, I can empathize with their fear. People can look like the most self-assured, polished speakers, but inside they may be terrified children.

Rande Davis Gedaliah is a principal in Gedaliah Communications of New York City, which offers keynotes, consulting, and seminars on "Speaking for Results."

THE ATTITUDE OF OPENNESS

Perhaps as important as the joys of sharing and of growing is the cultivation through public speaking of a wonderful openness toward new ideas and new people. The visitor to a Toastmasters club meeting or a meeting of the National Speakers Association—a chapter or a national convention—senses almost immediately that the room is filled with people who are intellectually alive, who care about each other, and who are open to the new information and new relationships that meeting will bring them. The encouragement that Toastmaster members freely offer each other, along with the thoughtful evaluations of their performances, opens them not only to sharper skills but also to growing friendships. The marketing and speaking advice NSA members freely share with each other is a source of amazement to people accustomed to trade associations in which mutual suspicion abounds. These speakers become open to each other, to new ideas, and to an enlarged view of their possibilities.

LANGUAGE SKILLS

The difference between the serious, intentional public speaker and everybody else who mounts the platform to speak is apparent most readily in the use of language. An audience senses almost immediately that one speaker is just talking and another is giving a speech. Since everybody talks, just about everybody who is not rendered mute by severe speech apprehension can get up and "say a few words." Some can even pull off a fairly lengthy address without boring or angering an audience. What sets apart the intentional speaker from the casual speaker is the ability to find the right words for the ideas or feelings being expressed.

People with highly developed verbal skills clearly have an advantage in becoming successful speakers. Precise, colorful language seems to come out of these people with a fluidity born in heaven. In most situations, they are halfway home to speaking effectiveness. In other situations, their flowing speech may be their enemy, simply not right for the audience in front of them. Adlai Stevenson could not gear down his patrician rhetoric to match the plain talk of Dwight Eisenhower, and partially for that reason, he lost the presidential election in 1952. Martin Luther King, Jr., on the other hand, carefully used his Boston University Ph.D. language with one audience and his country preacher language with another. With his passion for justice, he changed the world forever.

People with ordinary verbal skills may have to work harder at language. They may labor with great difficulty at keeping the speech outline in grammatically parallel form, using the dictionary of synonyms and antonyms, and searching for that colorful metaphor that will leave the audience breathless, but they can do it. If you are in this category, you will find that the hard work is worth it—if only for the satisfaction of achievement. No one is born a talented fashion designer or running back or surgeon, and no one is born with all the verbal skills needed for platform excellence. What we are all born with is the capacity to become what we can envision, and that includes the superb use of language.

LISTENING SKILLS

Long neglected in both public and private educational programs, listening skills now have to be taught to adults in business and the professions. Who knows how many sales have been lost, how many pills ingested by mistake, how many relationships broken because someone did not know how to listen?

How does the study of public speaking enrich listening skills? Since public speaking is an experience shared by speaker and listener, there has to be a mutuality of concern about the process. Unfortunately, audience members rarely have the opportunity to discern their part in the process, especially if they are a random audience—like a crowd gathered to hear a political campaigner or a breakout seminar of convention attendees. If, on the other hand, they are an ongoing, intentional audience like a college class or a worshipping congregation, they may receive some instruction on how to listen. A professor may give students some clues as to how to listen so as to gain the maximum return on their tuition dollars or to excel on their final exam. If a congregation is fortunate, a priest, minister, imam, or rabbi will occasionally preach a sermon on how to listen to a sermon.

Just as you learn from what you teach someone else, helping audience members develop listening skills will inevitably improve your own listening skills. You help them by modeling good listening, having attended to what the meeting planner told you about them and having chosen your materials and language accordingly. Your demeanor on the platform—consistent eye contact and adaptation to their mood—shows them how well you are listening to them as you speak. You may also incorporate into the speech the transitions that will help people listen more effectively—"Do you follow my reasoning here? . . . Am I making myself clear? . . . Look at the question in yet another way . . . Here's another example . . . Let's move on to the next idea." These phrases are not only classic ways of moving the subject along, they are also subtle techniques of training audiences in listening.

The speaker whose heart and mind are genuinely on the audience is likely to help that audience listen, perhaps doing it quite instinctively. What should be clear is that the speaker who helps people listen better becomes a better listener.

THINKING SKILLS

The most obvious benefit to you in the process of preparing to speak in public is the necessity of organizing information. For starters, every presentation has a beginning, a middle, and an end. You can organize the middle into chronological, geographical, topical, problem–solution, or some other order. Having devised a basic outline that makes sense for the topic and the audience, you can use a different system of organization for each of the main points. The thoughtful speaker, especially one who keeps developing new material, begins looking at the world with an organizer's eye:

- "That chair has three parts—legs, seat and back."
- "Let's define the problem before we talk about solutions."
- "We need to look at how the situation arose, what it looks like, and the options available."
- "Here are four considerations that we have to look at before we make a decision."

The speaker is also driven to consider the motive appeals that are available. Why, you ask, would my audience believe my ideas and follow my lead? What do I know about the reasons people respond to speakers? I know that they possess some basic physical needs, and I may be able to tie my agenda to those needs—to be safe from danger, for example. I know also that they function from strong social motives; they need and want approval. Will my speech be effective if I appeal to their need to conform to the norms of society, or to their drive to be successful, or to their creative urges? The questions of motive that each speaker needs to ask for each presentation inevitably become part of that speaker's psyche, enriching the speaker's ability to influence people in the wider community, the workplace, and the home.

Another way the serious speaker is learning to think is in determining the ways to use information as proof of an idea's adequacy. For example, you want to help the retail employees in your business audience to improve their customer service. They have had minimal or no training in the subject. You have time to deal with only one major idea—the importance of good customer service to the audience members' jobs. Should you start by asserting your main idea and then move to the information that illustrates your point—probably some stories of good and bad customer service? If so, you would be using deductive reasoning. Or should you ease into your talk with several stories that illustrate your basic idea, ending your presentation by asserting your belief in the importance of superb customer service for audience members who want to keep their jobs? You would be using inductive reasoning. The very awareness of how to reason from particulars to a general conclusion, or vice versa, is a mind-sharpening process, increasing the thinking skills of a speaker.

Also, a speaker learns to think more clearly when dealing with cause-and-effect reasoning. If, for example, you are advocating the drastic cutting of taxes in order to strengthen the economy, you need to defend the process by which consumers' higher spendable income will produce more and better-paying jobs. Whether your argument goes from cause to effect, effect to cause, or effect to effect, the very process of thinking through the best way to deal with your material makes you aware of the reasoning to which you are subjected by other speakers, advertisers, and the media.

Many people who study public speaking find that they have become clearer in their thinking almost without realizing it. They become the people employers will hire and pay generously. David Reed, director of recruiting for Anderson Consulting of Chicago, says, "We look for people who are smart. We look for someone who is a critical thinker, someone who examines the pros and cons of a decision before deciding."[1]

LEADERSHIP SKILLS

Leadership, it is said, begins with showing up. It continues, however, with the ability to articulate the concerns at hand and move people toward their goals. Indeed, one definition of leadership says that, in an unorganized group, whoever is talking at the moment is exercising leadership, and whoever is talking the most sense moves into ongoing leadership.

Aside from the personal characteristics that define leadership—integrity, vision, flexibility, etc.— the best leaders are usually the best communicators. It is hard to imagine a corporate president who stumbles and mumbles at a board of directors meeting, having forgotten what she was going to say. While not needing to be a spellbinding platform speaker, the person who runs almost any organization must be able to put ideas together in a coherent way and communicate them with words that achieve a clear end.

Does skill in public speaking lead to leadership? Not always. Too many variables affect the degree to which a person exercises leadership in a particular situation. If you want to be a leader, however, you must learn to speak clearly and persuasively. James Humes, a professional speaker and author, notes that the American Academy of Political Scientists called the Reagan presidency the most successful in getting its ideals carried out since Franklin D. Roosevelt, who was another master communicator. Humes writes,

> Reagan may not have been a hands-on administrator, but when the "Great Communicator" spoke, people did not sit on their hands. He motivated; he inspired; he led. What was his secret? Well, like Franklin Roosevelt and Winston Churchill, he knew the language of leadership.[2]

Without a doubt, the discipline of learning to speak in public fosters leadership qualities and skills. Take, for example, just one of the speech disciplines that a college instructor or a Toastmaster assignment may require you to study—the use of language. You will learn how to fashion figures of speech that will evoke images in the minds of your audience. Suppose you are speaking to a union gathering and you want to affirm the intelligence and good sense of your blue-collar audience members. You are aware that they are sometimes intimidated by their managers. Knowing their language for management, you say, "You may think the *suits* have all the power in this company, but I want you to know . . ." (*metonymy,* substituting the name of a particular item that stands for the whole person). The speaker who uses a figure of speech that evokes an image in audience members' minds enables them to experience reality in graphic terms and to respond favorably to that speaker. People will follow speakers whose language is clear, vigorous, strong, image-evoking, and especially entertaining. Conversely, the speaker who uses any word that comes along or starts every other sentence with "um," "now," or "OK" is far less likely to exert strong leadership.

I have just completed my CTM (Competent Toastmaster) award application form. Looking at the titles of the 10 speeches I presented during the past year was like reading an exciting chapter in my life story.

Joining the Federal Toastmasters club in Washington, D.C., was part of a much larger plan. My father had been an active Toastmaster throughout his career in Los Angeles, California. As a young girl, I recall "helping" him practice his speeches. He would stand in front of my mother's full-length sewing mirror practicing his delivery and gestures. At age six, I was his biggest booster and critic. Tuesday night was his club night. I always eagerly anticipated his return to see if he had won the notorious Yak-Yak award—a set of wind-up, plastic teeth carefully mounted on a wooden stand. In my adoring memory, he always won!

When I joined Toastmasters, I was White House Liaison for the U.S. Department of Transportation. I committed myself to a standing lunch date every Wednesday with other Toastmasters at the Department of Transportation. From that day forward, my skills, friendships, and professional development progressed rapidly.

Toastmasters has taught me to take risks. The journey to my CTM was filled with surprises. My final speech was the dry run for my nomination as the President of the National Women's Political Caucus. Toastmaster skills helped me make a positive impression on the 800 delegates attending our biennial convention. Today I am leading this national organization that is dedicated to the identification, training, and support of women candidates for elected and appointed positions at every level of government.

I have only one regret: I wish Dad was around to see me win the Yak-Yak award![3]

Anita Perez Ferguson is President of the National Women's Political Caucus in Washington, D.C.

NOTES

1. David Reed, "To Surprising Degree, They Get Jobs," *The Philadelphia Inquirer,* May 13, 1996, p. C3.

2. James C. Humes, *The Sir Winston Method: The Five Secrets of Speaking the Language of Leadership* (New York: William Morrow, 1991), p. 13.

3. Anita Perez Ferguson, *The Toastmaster,* December, 1995, p. 21.

3 Community Service

Speakers who find their way to the platforms provided by groups in their communities discover deep satisfaction in what they can bring to people. Their urge to communicate comes from deeply held values they want to share or from the belief that their knowledge will benefit their listeners. While these speakers have the same opportunity as every other citizen to communicate through conversations, writing letters and pamphlets, participating in broadcast talk shows, or writing books, they choose to stand in front of a group of people, look them in the eye, and communicate in what may be humankind's most personal and powerful way. Speaking to or on behalf of community groups provides pleasure and profit for both speaker and audience and enriches both.

How does public speaking enrich community? The word *communication* contains within it the word *community*—two words tightly related. Communication—whether involving two people or hundreds—creates community, but community also requires communication. In other words, when people communicate with each other, they are creating a community of persons—office staff, religious congregation, college class, Rotary Club, family. And if they are to survive as a community, those persons must communicate effectively with each other. If you define community as a town, village, or city, that place will certainly include some forms of communication called public speaking. It is hard to imagine a community without public speaking.

Occasionally, random groups form on a street corner to hear a political candidate, an advocate for a group of protesters, or an itinerant preacher, but most of the speaking in any town is done in the context of organized community groups. The entry point for persons who are serious about their calling to speak is the large assortment of people in every community who come together in groups of people having common interests. Who are these groups? What do they do? Which of them are looking for speakers? Which of them need someone to represent them to other segments of society?

Some groups, like military veterans, meet largely to socialize, while others meet to perform tasks together, like persons who package used clothing and household items for distribution by a charity. Still others meet to support each other in facing one of life's challenges—alcoholism, caregiving for elderly parents, starting a new business. These groups rarely, if ever, include a speaker in their group meetings.

Most groups, however, are also audiences for speakers. Perhaps at a yearly meeting they hear a report of the group's activities and the plans for the coming year. More often they meet weekly or monthly to renew their friendships, make decisions that advance their cause, and listen to an invited speaker.

SERVICE CLUBS

If you have driven into almost any small town in the United States, you have seen a collection of signs at its edges announcing the presence of its service clubs—Rotary, Kiwanis, and the like. The sign may even provide the time and place of meeting. Large city clubs may have a listing in the telephone directory. Each of these clubs meets weekly or bimonthly, almost always for a meal in a restaurant meeting room.

These clubs were organized by business and professional men but began to admit women into membership in the 1980s, thereby largely eliminating the parallel organizations women had developed, like the Lioness Clubs. The members enjoy each other's company and the opportunity for leadership and a good meal, but each has a charitable agenda. Rotary Clubs take a special interest in the community's youth, providing funds for school trips and college scholarships. Most Optimist clubs sponsor yearly public speaking contests for high school students, an excellent opportunity for Toastmasters and other serious speakers to gain experience acting as judges. The Lions Clubs have adopted eyesight as their project, sponsoring vision testing and collecting used eyeglasses for reuse. Sertoma Clubs take a special interest in people with hearing problems. The other service clubs—Kiwanis, Exchange, and others—pursue equally worthwhile goals.

The good news for budding speakers is that these clubs use a large number of speakers, sometimes one a week for 45 to 50 weeks in the year, and many communities nurture an abundance of these clubs. While their charitable interest may be sharply focused, their interest in speaking topics is quite broad. A program chair has a big job and is usually open to booking a speaker whose topic promises to be of some interest. Some clubs distribute the responsibility for finding speakers to several members, each of whom takes a one- or two-month period. In general, almost none of these groups pays a speaker, except perhaps for a district or regional gathering. If the speaker represents a needy cause, the group will sometimes make a contribution to that cause. If the speaker comes from a considerable distance just to address that club, it may reimburse transportation and lodging costs. Some clubs, like the Lions, are prevented by their charter from paying a speaking fee.

These service clubs engage many professional persons who speak about their specialties, such as chiropractors, financial planners, certified public accountants, psychotherapists, judges, and travel agents. They are also interested in hearing business leaders who can take them behind the scenes of their manufacturing plants or their software companies. They like to hear travelers who have visited famous or exotic places. They welcome securities traders, administrators of health-care facilities, representatives of local utilities, marriage and family counselors, school principals, college professors, genealogists, arborists, emergency medical technicians, athletes, and just about anyone else who can stretch their minds and expand their horizons.

RETIREES

Easily the fastest-growing segment of society, retired people are crowding senior clubs in ever-increasing numbers and forming new clubs all the time. For these groups, their primary common interest is their age and its implications for their lives. The American Association of Retired Persons (AARP), with more than 30 million members is the nation's largest group of seniors, asks only that its members have celebrated their 50th birthdays. Their age brings with it a list of concerns such as health care and changing relationships.

Older adults who are interested in speaking have abundant opportunities to provide leadership and to speak on behalf of the AARP's dozens of community-service activities. For example, the Grandparents Information Centers sponsor public awareness campaigns, alerting younger audiences to issues affecting grandparent caregiving and their linkages with aging, child, and family networks. Hundreds of seniors have volunteered as classroom instructors in the 55 Alive/Mature Driving program, an eight-hour classroom course for motorists 50 and older.

Other groups of retirees have more specific interests in common. The National Association of Retired Federal Employees is such a group. Members not only enjoy old times, many of them having worked together in the same government agencies, but also organize lobbying efforts to ensure their financial futures. The Telephone Pioneers welcome members who have served a given number of years for the phone company or who have reached a certain age. Many corporations having large numbers of former employees in one area sponsor regular meetings of their retirees. Speakers who can address the concerns of retired teachers are welcome at meetings of the twenty-six hundred chapters of the Retired Teachers Association. Some pay speakers; most do not. Life-care communities, many with hundreds of older people living in comfortable surroundings, convene to hear fine music, skilled entertainers, and informative speakers. Nearly all these communities welcome speakers who can enrich their lives, and many of them pay these speakers generously.

COLLEGE AND UNIVERSITY AUDIENCES

College and university students, faculty, and staff comprise one of the largest audience categories in the country. So sizable is the college speaking circuit that the National Association of Campus Activities sponsors a national convention and several regional gatherings every year to bring together speakers and performers of various kinds with deans and students who make decisions about campus programming. While celebrity speakers are popular choices, student groups and colleges themselves pay well to hear speakers who address important issues. Some of the larger speakers bureaus employ agents whose entire job is to book speakers into college and university venues.

Among the topics that college groups buy are those on accessibility for disabled persons, diversity, leadership, handling addictions, youth, violence and gangs, creative dating, the history and meaning of rock music, government today, living with AIDS, and immigration issues.

PROFESSIONAL GROUPS

Physicians, lawyers, architects, psychologists and other persons who have earned graduate degrees, who are offering their skills to the public, and who are certified by a state government licensing authority constitute a prime market for speakers. Their local associations generally meet monthly, with state, regional, and national meetings occurring every year. While they tend to program their own members as speakers—or peers from another geographic area—they frequently invite speakers and trainers who can help them increase their effectiveness. Most states require professional persons to take a certain number of continuing education hours to retain their licenses. Most associations themselves also require members to keep updating their knowledge and skills.

Speakers to professional groups, however, do not necessarily speak on technical subjects such as changing tax laws and new techniques in craniofacial surgery. Lay speakers offer such popular "soft topics" as time management, customer service, coping with change, and handling stress. Like almost every organization, professional groups are pleased to have competent speakers who do not charge them, but most are prepared to offer a generous fee for work well done. Many professional speakers have cultivated one or more such associations as highly profitable niche markets, speaking to dozens of regional and state conventions over a period of years.

BUSINESS ORGANIZATIONS

People in business get together in a variety of ways for a variety of reasons. When they do, they spend considerable time listening to speakers. Their gatherings may involve anything from a handful of people in one member's board room to tens of thousands in the vastness of Chicago's McCormick Place.

Among business gatherings, trade associations probably involve the largest number of people. Whether the trade is defined narrowly, like the Sciota County Kitchen and Bath Association, or broadly, like the National Association of Manufacturers, one program constant at association meetings is a speaker. At last count, the American Society of Association Executives (ASAE) included about twenty-four thousand members who manage leading business, professional, educational, technical, industrial, and trade associations. Its ten thousand associations serve more than 287 million people and companies. The vast majority of associations employ speakers at their meetings.

Ken Sommer, an executive with the ASAE, says that while corporations pay an enormous amount of money for meetings, "associations are a major player in hiring speakers," noting a study that found that 44 percent of the ASAE associations recently surveyed had hired three or more speakers per convention. About 47 percent had paid between $2,000 and $5,000 per speaker.[1]

Best known to the public among business groups are the Chambers of Commerce. About seven thousand of them in the United States meet to advance the cause of business, some highly staffed with huge budgets and others that are part-time operations managed by one member as a sideline. They work with government and other civic organizations to advance the general interests of their communities and especially to create a quality of life that will attract investment and job-generating enterprises to their area.

A fairly recent phenomenon among business gatherings is the local networking or lead-generating meeting. One of them advertises in a suburban weekly: "The Leads Club, a professional business networking organization, is looking for members, Wednesdays, 7:00 P.M., in the Broomall area. Call [phone]." A metropolitan Union League club sponsors a business network, using occasional speakers, as does the Jewish Business Network in the same city, featuring a monthly speaker who makes a presentation after people have introduced themselves and their businesses.

LIBRARIES, BOOKSTORES, AND DEPARTMENT STORES

Many libraries that have sponsored reading clubs for children and adults have been adding a widening variety of programs that fit the public's hunger for continuing education opportunities. Libraries that can rearrange their furniture to accommodate an audience frequently invite teachers, local authors, consultants, and others to speak on their specialties or to conduct series of seminars.

Larger bookstores, especially those operated by national chains, use local experts on topics of general interest as a marketing tool to bring people into their stores. They may also use a local author or one coming through town on a book promotion tour, featuring an autographing session and a discount on the book. Sometimes they invite a local expert on the topic of a current best-seller to offer a review and critique of that book.

In a recent month, Borders, a large suburban bookstore in Springfield, Pennsylvania, welcomed speakers on these topics:

- The Insider's Guide to Buying Home Furnishings
- Everything You Always Wanted to Know about Classical Music but Were Afraid to Ask
- Caring for Your Pet
- Alternative Medicine: Changing Our Concept of Illness and Health

- The Art and Life of Paul Cézanne
- Empowerment and the Mind's Role in Health and Healing
- Changes: A Self-Help Book for Adolescents (by Harry Vincenzi)
- Retired and Senior Volunteer Program
- The Joy of Writing Sex (by Elizabeth Benedict)
- The Ramadan Sonnets—Poetry by Daniel Moore
- Chronic Illness and the Family (by Linda Welsh)
- Big Brother/Big Sister

Boscov's, a large department store chain on the Eastern seaboard, runs an extensive program of several dozen popular courses ranging from astrology to financial planning to parenting—a project of the store's marketing department. Large numbers of people who would not otherwise enter the store enroll for those courses (and may buy some products on their way in or out!). The store even offers a discount for persons paying the modest course fees with the store credit card. Instructors receive a small honorarium and may use their participation as a marketing tool for their own businesses.

RESIDENTIAL ORGANIZATIONS

Renters in large apartment complexes, condominium owners, and residents of gated communities may sponsor a variety of activities—theater jaunts, trips to gaming centers, and on-site concerts and lectures. Their activities committee or a staff person welcomes speakers who can provide valuable information to these audiences, such as personal security or financial planning principles, sometimes paying them very well. Also welcome are entertainers, humorists, or speakers whose material has a high entertainment value.

FRATERNAL ORGANIZATIONS

The Masonic order leads any list of fraternal organizations in terms of numbers of members. Some men belong only to the basic organization, the Blue Lodge; others add memberships in corollary organizations, including the Order of the Eastern Star, the majority of whose members are women. Other fraternal groups, most of them organized to provide inexpensive insurance for their members and their children, include the Moose, the Elks, and the Oddfellows. Most of these groups, now declining in membership, spend their meeting time in performing their rituals, doing the business that carries out their purposes, and enjoying their bonds of friendship. It is the rare fraternal organization that engages a speaker, but those that do constitute a friendly and respectful audience.

CHARITABLE AND NONPROFIT ORGANIZATIONS

While groups committed to charitable causes sometimes welcome speakers from the community, the nature of their work is more likely to put them on the giving side of the speaking equation. Most of the major national organizations dedicated to health causes sponsor people who will speak on their behalf to service clubs and other audiences. In-house speakers bureaus have been formed as an important promotional tool for local and regional units of such groups as the American Heart Association, the American Cancer Society, the American Red Cross, and the American Lung Association. Lower profile groups concerned with less well-known diseases such as lupus, multiple sclerosis, and hearing loss may also provide speakers to community groups. Many busy professional speakers have begun their careers as volunteer speakers for one of these charities.

Other nonprofits also use speakers to get their messages out to the public, for operating funds, and for support to influence legislation. The John Howard Society concerns itself with prison reform. Greenpeace is one of the better-known organizations promoting the preservation of the environment. Nearly every community has a right-to-life organization and a pro-choice group. The National Rifle Association gladly encourages its members to articulate the group's cause, as do organizations dedicated to banning handguns and assault rifles. A person who wishes to gain speaking experience, especially one who is passionate about one of these causes, may well volunteer to speak on behalf of a nonprofit group.

POLITICAL ORGANIZATIONS

Political organizations are also designed to supply speakers rather than to be spoken to. The opportunities to speak on behalf of a political party are somewhat rare for a noncandidate compared to the opportunities for speaking on behalf of a nonprofit group. Service clubs are wary of political speakers unless candidates themselves are willing to appear on a panel, in a debate, or in a series of talks that include speakers from opposing parties. Nevertheless, a noncandidate may appear at political meetings as a master of ceremonies for a candidate, representing the views of the voters of a particular community and introducing the candidate to the audience. The person who works hard as a township commissioner or party secretary and speaks up at meetings may well develop such a rapport with political audiences as to become the candidate in the next election. That process has produced a great many state and national political leaders.

WOMEN'S CLUBS

Women's clubs are in a serious state of decline, the average age of their membership now in the 60s and rising every year. Today's economic climate has sent large numbers of women into the workforce, excluding them from the leisurely daytime meetings that once attracted large numbers of women. Some women's clubs have fought back by changing their meeting times to the evening hours, but working women with children find it just as difficult to attend those meetings. Women's clubs welcome speakers on a wide variety of subjects, paying them comparatively small amounts. Some clubs, especially those affiliated with the General Federation of Women's Clubs, combine forces to conduct area auditions attended by the women who plan the programs. This group issues a list of available speakers for their clubs, most of whom speak free or for less than $100.

Women's clubs whose purposes are more targeted are also suffering. Garden, writer's, music, and art clubs are drawing ever-smaller numbers of women, most of them at retirement age. If they use any speakers, they generally invite their own members or persons in their communities who share their interests. Parent groups, usually made up by a majority of women, invite speakers, especially when the group functions under the auspices of schools that can swell the audience with teachers and can help provide a fee.

Today's most vigorous women's groups are those committed to defining and expanding the role of women in business and the professions. Two major national organizations sponsor most of the local and regional clubs: The National Federation of Business and Professional Women's Clubs, which has twenty-two hundred local groups involving seventy thousand members, and the American Businesswomen's Association, which has ninety thousand members in sixteen hundred local chapters. Local chapters may or may not pay their speakers; regional and national conventions are likely to pay generously.

SUPPORT GROUPS

Support groups bring together people who need each other for mutual support, encouragement, and healing. The community calendar section of just about any weekly newspaper lists meetings of such groups as Alcoholics Anonymous (AA), Male Partners of Women in Recovery, Take Off Pounds Sensibly (TOPS), Single Moms in Loving Encouragement (SMILE), Mothers Against Drunk Driving (MADD), Alzheimer's Caregivers, and Multiple Sclerosis Support Group. By their very nature, support groups channel their energy and dues payments into members helping each other. Some engage a speaker for their monthly meetings; some may ask a specialist in the area of their interest to address an annual gathering to which the members invite guests; but most meet year after year without hearing any speakers at all. Speakers who are hired by the few groups that offer a fee find that it is a modest one and accept it graciously; others return it to the group and claim it as a charitable income tax deduction.

In Appendix F, you will find a list that suggests the kinds of organizations in your community that may be open to having you as a speaker.

NOTE

1. Fannie Weinstein, "Professionally Speaking," *Profiles*, April 1995, p. 52.

4 Vocational Fulfillment

Speaking in public is a part of the job description for a great many people. While no one speaks from a platform 40 hours a week, the presentations that people make as an integral part of their work often define both their identity and their success. By vocational fulfillment, I refer to people whose paychecks come to them in part because they successfully communicate their messages to appropriate audiences as speakers. For them, speaking is simply a part of their job; it comes with the territory. The people discussed in this chapter would not usually describe themselves as professional speakers, although much of their time is spent on their feet making presentations. While speaking to groups is important to them, they are unlike (1) speakers who are paid almost exclusively for their speaking skills—lecturers and motivational speakers, (2) avocational speakers—professional and business leaders who speak as a second income enterprise, and (3) sponsored speakers. Each of these will be discussed in later chapters.

If you are studying public speaking in a college class or participating in a Toastmasters club—or you are a working person considering a vocational change that would enable you to use your speaking skills to earn a living—the job categories that follow may help you think through your options.

EDUCATORS

People who teach are on their feet, talking, for a substantial part of every day. Most elementary school teachers have one audience all day long, five days a week. They do not usually think of themselves as public speakers, except perhaps when they address a parent–teacher audience. However, they use most of the techniques required of all speakers: developing reliable sources of information, organizing their material in ways that their audiences can understand, using language that makes sense to their listeners, and skillfully putting to use their voices and bodies.

Middle and secondary school teachers come closer to the category of public speaking since they are specialists, usually talking about one subject—history, English, computer science, or chemistry, for example. In addition, their students are able to handle longer presentations of information than are elementary school students. Teachers who communicate their subject matter with a high degree of speaking skill are greatly appreciated by both their students and their administrators. When they add to their speaking skills the use of visual aids and creatively involve their students in discussions and projects, they are regarded as outstanding teachers.

College and university professors in many fields are expected to become expert stand-up communicators, and many are among the most highly skilled speakers in our society. Undergraduate classes in many required subjects may enroll several hundred students arrayed in a large lecture hall, where the primary means of learning is listening to a lecture. These professors may actually be communicating to many times the number of people they can see, through video channels to classes on campuses many miles away and on videotapes to be seen later by significant numbers of adult learners. These same professors may also be in demand for presentations to various business groups, trade associations, community audiences, and students on other campuses.

Not to be forgotten are some of the most eloquent of university faculty, the athletic coaches, whose half-time oratory has enlivened many a disheartened team to win a seemingly hopeless game. It should not be surprising that many of them have transferred their oratorical ability to the business platform—especially those who have moved on to coaching professional teams—earning as much from a couple of speeches on the business platform as their annual university salary.

Professors who have moved into administrative posts find themselves on many platforms. In both small colleges and huge universities, provosts, deans, admission officers, directors of student services, and department heads generally find themselves speaking to student groups, to employees, and even to community organizations when issues arise that affect the college's wider locale. The president or chancellor is expected to bring highly developed speaking skills to fulfilling frequent demands for public appearances before student and community groups—and in the case of tax-supported colleges, before state legislatures and their committees.

BROADCASTERS AND JOURNALISTS

The worlds of radio, television, and the print media are filled with people who have studied speech communication. Many college and university speech communication departments offer specialized courses in broadcasting and journalism. Many larger institutions make available a major in that field. Some schools combine courses in broadcasting and journalism to form a major called broadcast journalism. The facilities for broadcasting courses range from fairly simple studios converted from unused basement rooms to free-standing buildings sophisticated enough to house a public television station.

Professors qualify for their faculty posts by having gained extensive experience in commercial or educational broadcasting. Most have also earned graduate degrees and are teaching full-time, while adjunct instructors are currently making their livings in their fields of expertise.

Public speaking courses are valuable for people who enter broadcasting and journalism, with or without a major in communications. The skill of focusing on a specific subject, researching it, and putting the information into coherent, interesting language is central to broadcasters and journalists as well as to speakers.

POLITICAL LEADERS

Every four years, nearly everybody in the United States becomes a rhetorical critic, evaluating the speaking ability of the presidential candidates. For a while, they do what students and professors of rhetoric do every day in the classroom. In every boutique, barber shop, and bar, people freely share their opinions about the length, language, and impact of the presidential candidate they saw on television the night before. The universality of these analyses, however simplistic and uninformed, are honest responses to what people have heard. They testify to the role that public speaking plays in our democratic society.

Campaigning for office at every level of government requires candidates to tell voters what they believe and how they plan to represent their constituents if elected to office. From school board member to candidate for the United States Congress, political hopefuls must work public speaking into their campaign strategy. That speaking may involve talking with a handful of people who are sitting around a citizen's kitchen table or giving a formal address to a black-tie audience gathered for a $1,000-a-plate fund-raiser at a four-star hotel.

The setting is incidental to the speaker's agenda: to convey information and ideas persuasively, organized carefully, and delivered skillfully. An occasional candidate may be elected largely through an expensive, slick television advertising campaign but will not remain in office long without the ability to meet with constituents and talk to them face-to-face, frequently as a public speaker.

ATTORNEYS

Not all attorneys address juries and judges. But the lawyers who do speak in courtroom settings, called trial lawyers, make a significant contribution both to their clients and to the legal system. Few of them speak with the eloquence of a William Jennings Bryan, a Perry Mason, or a Johnny Cochran. But eloquence is neither the primary goal nor the method of today's courtroom attorneys. Rather, attorneys who hope to win their cases commit their prime energy to the evidence and logic of their cases. They also give considerable weight to audience analysis, sometimes engaging psychologists to provide profiles of potential jurors and witnesses. If, in addition to these factors, they can use incisive and colorful language and manage their voices and bodies skillfully, they are highly successful advocates.

It would be a mistake to indicate that only trial lawyers need to concern themselves with the skills of public speaking. People generally perceive lawyers as people who think and speak clearly. Citizens call on them to speak to schools and other civic groups. When a business engages a lawyer to represent its interests, that work may well involve speaking to an audience of people gathered to protest a corporate policy, the governing body of a nonprofit association, or a zoning board. Cases are sometimes won or lost not on the evidence alone but on the speaking ability of the attorney.

TRAINERS

The mobility of the workforce and ever-changing technology in the United States require constant training in businesses of every size. While some training involves one-on-one guidance in an on-the-job setting, much of it involves a stand-up communicator in a training classroom. For persons in the training business, public speaking skills are indispensable.

The question is frequently asked, what is the difference between training and public speaking? It is a question that motivational speakers wrestle with when they are asked to take their standard keynote speech into a company's training room, narrowed or expanded for a particular group of employees and spread out over a day or two. Likewise, trainers get requests to condense their material into a half-hour keynote speech for a large state or national convention audience.

> Why did I want to make the switch from trainer to keynote speaker? I felt I had the ability to get a clear, hard-hitting message across in a short period of time. I also felt I could get people to respond and act on that message. While the evaluations on my seminars had always been good, things such as audience participation were never my strong suit. I also enjoy developing stories much more than developing training exercises. . . . In today's competitive environment, you have to deliver an equally good message and as much content in an hour as you would in a half or full day, while motivating and entertaining at the same time.
>
> **Warren Greshes** is a busy keynote speaker from New York City who began his speaking career as a trainer. His article "From Trainer to Keynote Speaker" appears in *Professional Speaker,* September 1996.

Most of the differences Warren Greshes notes in his first-person story suggest at least part of the answer to the question, how does training differ from speaking? The best answer is to be found not in sharp distinctions between speaking and training but along a continuum between the two activities. Because so many speakers also function as trainers and because meeting planners are not always clear as to which service they are buying, it is important to look closely at both the overlapping and the distinctions between these categories. Sometimes it strains even the experienced observer's ability to decide if the presenter is training or speaking.

The following table lists eight categories that pertain to presentations in general—both speaking and training—each of which may facilitate an understanding of the similarities and differences between these two activities.

	Training	**Speaking**
Goal	Facilitate learning	Inform, motivate
Time	Generous	Compressed
Audience	Smaller	Larger
Materials	Content rich	Less content rich
	Expository, straightforward	Narrative, figurative
	Workbook, handouts	No workbook
	Cognitive/Behavioral	Affective/Cognitive
Organization	Clear, linear	Less apparent
Visuals	Expected	Optional
Results	Measurable	Hopeful
Rewards	Less money per hour	More money per hour

A discussion follows for each of these categories that will help to clarify the differences between speaking and training.

The Goal

A trainer is a facilitator of learning. The trainer's goal is to help listeners absorb and understand new information or to recall information that people possess but are not utilizing. Furthermore, many trainers are given the assignment to change the skill levels of participants or to modify their behavior in some important way. Speakers, on the other hand, are usually less intentional about changing specific behaviors. They present new or neglected information or motivational material—always with a creative twist and usually with strong entertainment value. They aim to change people for the good, but rarely with the clear expectation of measurable change.

The Time

Trainers generally have a relatively large amount of time for their work compared to speakers. A trainer may consume anywhere from half a day to three or four days to cover the appropriate material. A speaking engagement is more likely to range from 30 to 90 minutes. Many full-time professional speakers are keenly aware of this distinction when they fulfill dual assignments for a multiday convention, delivering a keynote address (speaking) and doing two or three breakout sessions (training).

The Audience

If a presenter's goal is to produce significant change in peoples' behavior, not only must the time available be generous but also the audience must be relatively small. Audience members are more likely to become involved in some activity and to enjoy substantial time for questions. While a speaker before a large audience may produce some limited audience involvement, it is much more difficult. So also is the handling of questions from a large number of people. In general, a trainer will face audiences from 6 to 60 people, a speaker from 50 to 1,000 or more.

The Materials

Content Rich versus Less Content Rich

While a speaker's material is expected to be content rich, many professional speakers make a good living with fairly thin content, especially if their forte is humor or motivation. For a trainer to skimp on the content of the presentation is unthinkable. One kind of motivational speaker may fill 80 percent to 90 percent of the available time with narratives of people, corporations, or associations that have been successful. The remaining 10 percent to 20 percent of the time may produce some important principles or articulate some techniques that account for that success. Humorists employ one-liners or a succession of humorous narratives to make a point—if a point is made at all. What humorists and motivational speakers do is not at all inappropriate—depending on the audience and its expectations. Their work represents a highly respectable genre of professional speaking. It is in great demand and is highly rewarded. On the other hand, many professional speakers are very content rich and use humor sparingly. They pepper their speech with just the right amount of entertaining material to convey their ideas in a pleasant and memorable way. Audiences expect trainers to be interesting, but they are not strongly disappointed if there is no humor and relatively little entertainment value.

Expository versus Narrative

The ratio between an expository approach with straightforward language and a narrative approach with figurative language suggests another distinction between training and speaking. Speakers are much more likely to convert expository material into narrative than are trainers. The *trainer* may say, "There are four areas an employer must not inquire about when interviewing candidates for a job: (1) marital status, (2) religious faith, (3) political affiliation, and (4) sexual preference," and then proceed to explain the reasons they are both inappropriate and illegal. The *speaker* is more likely to call these four items "No-No Territory" and relay an attention-compelling story about an employer who was unaware of this forbidden forest and got caught in the thicket of government censure and penalty. In this example, notice how the speaker relies on metaphors to make the point. The ideas may be roughly the same but the styles are quite different.

Like the other areas in which training and speaking occupy different points on the continuum, these distinctions with regard to speech material and style are suggestive and not definitive. Some individual trainers are highly imaginative and creative and some speakers are quite linear and straightforward, but the distinction, on the whole, seems to be a valid one.

Workbook and Handouts

Another difference is that the materials covered by the trainer are more likely to be given to participants in a workbook or in a batch of handouts. Trainers may even direct their listeners to take notes or fill in some blanks. The people who hire speakers do not normally expect them to rely heavily on printed resources, though some speakers do use printed material quite successfully.

Cognitive/Behavioral versus Affective/Cognitive

The final distinction to be drawn about the use of materials may be the most telling: training leans heavily toward the cognitive and behavioral domains and speaking toward the affective—but not without a cognitive dimension. The proof is to be found in audience comments after presentations by both trainers and speakers at the same convention, some vocally and others in writing. The persons hired as speakers are described in terms such as: "inspirational" . . . "I'll never be the same" . . . "highly motivating" . . . "exciting" . . . I laughed so hard I cried." Trainers get comments that express appreciation: "I learned so many new things" . . . "I can take this information back to the office and really use it" . . . "The instructor opened my eyes to a whole new world."

The Organization

Participants in a training session expect the material to have a clear, linear structure. They want to go home with lists of principles, steps, cautions, techniques, or whatever ideas the trainer has conveyed to them. They are helped when they can discern the outline of the material in major and minor categories. They want to remember what was covered.

The speaker will also have carefully organized the material to be presented, but the outline is less likely to be apparent to the audience. The speaker is usually less concerned that the audience retain information than that they feel something strongly. The speaker is less likely to use a "firstly, secondly, and thirdly" approach than is the trainer, because remembering is less important than experiencing.

The Visuals

While the use of overhead transparencies, slides, flip charts, models, and other visual aids has long been a staple of trainers, the differences between trainers and speakers in the use of visuals is rapidly eroding. The advent of less expensive visual aids generated by computer software is making visuals extremely popular with presenters of all kinds, including motivational speakers. Multimedia presentations, some quite spectacular, are becoming the common currency of many professional speakers.

What has not changed, however—and will never change—is the power of the lone speaker with no visual aids at all. Attendees at a recent convention of the National Speakers Association will never forget the spine-tingling keynote address by Gerry Coffee, who told of his experience as one of the longest-held POWs in North Vietnam. Charts of the number of American prisoners taken or pictures of his prison camp would have been ludicrously out of place in that presentation. Words alone conveyed almost more than the audience could handle, and words alone will continue to captivate and move audiences. Any speaker who will pay the price of finding the right word for the right idea or emotion will always be in demand.

The Results

Who knows with any finality what happens to the words sent into an audience by a presenter? Trainers are more likely to find out than speakers. People who employ trainers are disposed to require written evaluations to a far greater extent than are those who hire speakers. If speakers indeed work in the affective domain to a greater extent than do trainers, it follows that knowing the results is a far more difficult task. One can test the new skills or the comprehension and retention of data that is the trainer's responsibility to convey, but how does one test or measure the feelings the speaker works to arouse? And how important is it to know?

The Rewards

Professional speakers tend to believe that they will earn more money per minute on the platform as speakers than they will as trainers. Therefore the corridor conversations among attendees at the National Speakers Association and the American Society for Training and Development abound with talk about moving from training to speaking and especially to keynote speaking, in which the platform time expended is low and the fees are high but the competition is extremely stiff. Warren Greshes counters this assumption: "You can make as much, if not more, money in the training and consulting business as you can in keynoting. You can make money doing anything if you're good at it and really love doing it."[1]

Increasingly, presenters are functioning as both speakers and trainers, depending on the needs of the meeting planner for a particular event. Persons with skill in public speaking can easily adapt to the buyer's needs, one time functioning as a speaker and another time as a trainer.

MARKETERS

Marketing functions somewhere between the availability of a product or service and the purchase of it. Marketing calls to prospects' attention the identity of what is being offered so that a sale can be made expeditiously. Perhaps no area of business has attracted more attention in recent decades than marketing. Books, consultants, and college majors have surfaced in staggering numbers to define the field and its techniques. In addition to the billions of dollars spent every year on marketing, millions are spent on research about marketing.

Little noticed in the marketing mix, but of genuine significance, is the role of public speaking. While not a large role as compared to the money spent on advertising and publicity, marketing is done by two kinds of speakers, (1) corporate marketers and (2) free-lancers.

Corporate Marketers

Employees of pharmaceutical companies, such as registered pharmacists and medical doctors, make themselves available for major addresses or breakout sessions at meetings of health professionals—especially the ones attended by persons responsible for ordering pharmaceutical products. Their presentations are designed to raise the awareness of potential buyers to medicines they may eventually be able to prescribe. More will be said about this in the section on sponsored speakers in Chapter 8.

Another vocational group that uses public speaking as a marketing tool is the financial services industry. A firm of financial planners, for example, may sponsor a free seminar to which it invites the prospects developed by its partners and associates or one advertised to the general public. A speaker outlines the reasons people should concern themselves with intelligent planning of their financial future—for sending their children to college and for retiring comfortably. The speaker asks for an evaluation at the end of the seminar. The final question is, Would you like a free, confidential one-hour consultation about your financial situation? Those who agree and return for that consultation become prospects for an ongoing, in-depth series of fee-paid sessions to help them identify and achieve their financial objectives. Another firm may sponsor a seminar to inform clients and potential clients about investments in stocks and bonds.

These examples may sound like obvious, straightforward, commercial efforts—and some are—but most of this marketing is quite subtle. References to any product or service are usually well hidden in an abundance of genuinely useful information. Opportunities are sometimes given that lead directly to selling situations, with brokers or consultants following up the seminar by phoning attendees. At other times, firms are content just to make a positive impression about their companies.

Free-Lance Marketers

Free-lance marketers operate in a variety of ways. Sometimes they are contracted to slip into their otherwise commercial-free presentations the name of a sponsoring company. Patricia Gallagher, a speaker from Bucks County, Pennsylvania, recently did a book tour featuring her self-published book on child rearing. She scheduled the tour during the school vacation period and took her children on the road, contracting with Holiday Inns for their lodging and meals. During her speeches she referred to the Holiday Inn hotel chain as an example of an unusually family-friendly environment. In some cases she also received a fee. Steven Newman, journalist-author of *Worldwalking,* a book chronicling his four-year walk around the world, speaks on behalf of the Ohio Apple Marketing Program. As an authentic Ohio folk hero known by the weekly dispatches he sent to Ohio newspapers during his travels, he speaks to schools and community groups using the stories of another Ohio folk hero, Johnny Appleseed. Another form of free-lance marketing is the heavily advertised, free weekend workshops promoted by real estate entrepreneurs who tell their audiences how they can make money by buying and reselling foreclosed property.

SALESPERSONS

With increasing frequency, people who sell high-price goods or services are making their presentations to groups. Buying decisions that involve large sums of money or that affect a diverse group of people require the input of the stakeholders involved.

The process of preparing and making a sales presentation to a buying group is virtually identical to the speech-making process: analyzing the audience to be able to discern its needs and speak its language, organizing well-researched material, and optimizing the resources of voice, body, and visuals.

An even closer consonance between speaker and salesperson lies in the classical concept of "the good person speaking well." In recent years the field of sales has been moving away from the "Red-Hot, Cold Call Selling" approach. Top-notch salespeople have taken a second look at their sales pitches, objection-handling skills, and closing techniques. They are moving toward developing strong, positive relationships with prospects and purchasers, doing what is now called consultative selling. Today's salespeople, even in retailing, are learning to build bridges of friendship with their customers.

What today's salespeople have discovered is that Aristotle's concept of *ethos* lies at the very heart of persuasive communication. No matter how carefully crafted the data, the stories, the pauses, and the laugh lines, there will be no sale if the presenter appears to be lacking in competence, integrity, and goodwill. If the salesperson builds on that fundamental principle and, in addition, honestly uses the elements of *pathos,* enabling prospects to visualize the product or service in action—even to experience it viscerally—the sale is just about made. It is then that Aristotle's third means of persuasion, the *logos*—the data itself—makes sense to the prospective buyer and becomes the final element that wraps up the deal.

MANAGERS

Managers make their livings by talking, most often to the people they supervise. While most of the talking may be one-on-one, managers are always running group meetings. In those groups, managers lay out plans for the week's work, explain new corporate policy, and attempt to motivate their people to higher levels of achievement. Association executives update their boards of directors on developing plans for the next annual convention. Nursing home administrators outline the agenda for securing accreditation. School principals inform teachers about new guidelines being imposed by the state secretary of education.

Just about every one of the learning assignments given to a Speech 101 student or to a Toastmaster working toward the Competent Toastmaster award will be useful in a management job. Every manager alive, from the CEO of a Fortune 500 company to the night supervisor of a warehouse security squad, needs the skills of a public speaker.

CLERGY

Worshippers in church or synagogue are likely to experience a form of public speaking called preaching. The ordained persons who do it—priests, imams, ministers, and rabbis—have studied the discipline called *homiletics*, a word derived from both Greek and Latin words that refers to religious gatherings. Its apparent definition is that preaching is public speaking on religious themes. In one sense, that is a clear and obvious definition, but for most denominations, preaching in the Christian tradition has taken on a more sharply focused meaning: the proclamation of the good news of God's creative and redeeming love in Jesus Christ and the meaning of that love for the individual and for the world. In the Jewish tradition, preaching points to the activity of God in Israel's history and its life today; God's marvelous gift of the Law; and the importance of increasing love for God and humankind through obedience to the Scriptures. As a rapidly growing Islamic movement has come to the attention of the West through television and the mosques beginning to dot cities throughout the United States, people are being exposed to preaching by Muslim religious leaders called imams, who base their sermons on the Koran, exalting Allah and calling believers to holy living.

COMMUNITY ACTIVISTS

The category of community activist includes people with a wide variety of identities and agendas. The street preacher may not be an ordained person but is certainly communicating a message to the community with a passion for its improvement. The bullhorn-toting leader of objectors to increased utility rates may gather some folk at the doors of the state regulatory commission office and make a strong, reasoned case—perhaps even winning the argument with the authorities. Other speakers serve their communities in tamer surroundings—the labor union president who speaks persuasively to a corporate executive committee and earns important concessions in the labor contract, or the president of the ballet troupe's governing board who persuades a charitable foundation's executive committee to make a major grant.

Every citizen of this free country who believes strongly in a worthwhile cause and who can bring competent speech-making skills to that cause is fulfilling the clearest and strongest dream of its founders and of one of its greatest presidents, Abraham Lincoln, who demonstrated by his own platform skills how to make ours a government "of the people, by the people, and for the people."

NOTE

1. Warren Greshes, "From Trainer to Keynote Speaker: Making the Switch," *Professional Speaker*, September 1996, p. 6.

Learning and Teaching

Americans invest a prodigious amount of time, energy, and money into learning to speak in public. Learners generally require teachers. Who those learners are and who the teachers are—and how they find each other—is the subject of this chapter.

People interested in public speaking will see themselves in one or both of two roles: a learner or a teacher. Every one of the educational settings described in this chapter provides an opportunity to learn the communication skills necessary to speak in front of an audience. Likewise, every one provides opportunity for people skilled in public speaking to share their knowledge and expertise with others. Somewhere in these settings you are likely to find where you belong in the public speaking enterprise—perhaps in just one place where you need to be right now, and quite likely in other places as you develop your insights and skills.

ELEMENTARY SCHOOLS

Public speaking in elementary schools may seem to begin and end with the show-and-tell period in the earliest grades or the traditional presentation of the "What I Did on My Summer Vacation" talk. Actually, elementary school students may get considerable experience by making oral reports of their science experiments or their observations of wildlife, ocean tides, and the variety of cloud formations. Groups of students sometimes form a panel to communicate to the class what they learned about a period in history. The pedagogical emphasis is, as it should be, on the content and organization of the material rather than on its delivery. But what elementary school students learn about responsible research and clear organization of ideas is basic to all public speaking, wherever else that skill may subsequently be developed. Teachers who are intentional about the values of public speaking may also help students develop high standards of diction, eye contact, and other speaking skills.

Another area in which elementary school pupils may develop their communication skills is in listening. While good listening is taught implicitly by good teachers throughout the instructional process, it may be taught explicitly using a wide variety of learning materials that are in the market.

SECONDARY SCHOOLS

Many high schools provide abundant opportunity to develop public speaking skills. Others give it virtually no attention at all aside from the oral reports students may give in the course of learning. The schools between these extremes generally offer a public speaking unit of at least a few weeks. In one outstanding school, the Upper Darby High School in Pennsylvania, ninth graders begin the year with a nine-week module called core skills, designed to prepare them for the last four years of required education. Students are given an important issue to research in teams of three. They must work together to gain some experience in using library resources, to organize what they learned, and to share the information with the class in a panel. Each student then gives a brief solo presentation on one aspect of the data. At the junior-senior level, they may elect a research and communication course in which they will read and analyze famous speeches, debate the issues involved on material they have developed in their collateral reading, and give an original speech in which they take a stand.

Some high schools offer an elective in business communication, usually in the nonacademic track, whose course outline includes both writing and speaking skills. Several state departments of education are now requiring a senior project that requires for graduation a major research effort resulting in (1) a term paper; (2) a production of some sort that grows out of the research—a demonstration, a play, a piece of music, or a speech; and (3) an oral report to a panel of state-approved judges who will certify that the student is literate enough to deserve a high school diploma. Some secondary schools sponsor intercollegiate forensic teams who compete in such areas as debate, oratory, and the oral interpretation of literature; some assign speechwriting projects, exercises in rhetorical criticism, and even persuasive speaking.

COLLEGES AND UNIVERSITIES

A high percentage of the more than four thousand institutions of higher learning offers some help in speech communication to students who want to develop an understanding about the role speech plays in society and to develop their skills. For both speech majors and those studying in other disciplines, a variety of speech communications courses are offered: organizational communications, interpersonal communications, communication science and disorders, oral interpretation, argumentation and debate, mass communications, and theater. Public speaking, however, is an almost universal offering at the college level.

Many people who have never gone to college as well as those who have graduated have abundant opportunities to draw on the resources of colleges and universities. Community colleges, formerly called junior colleges, offer approximately the same variety of courses students might find in the first two years of a four-year college or university. Students who complete the two years generally earn an Associate in Arts (A.A.) degree and may easily move on to the last two years of a four-year college. Even those who take one year or less may also transfer to another college. The minimal speech course offering is generally limited to basic speech communication, almost always with a public speaking unit. Some community colleges offer a communication arts major including courses called introduction to oral communication, voice enhancement, small group communication, argumentation and debate, public speaking, and interviewing skills.

One of the first places to look for evening courses in any community is its community college, since its charter generally calls for a rich program of evening and weekend courses to serve the needs of the communities whose tax money provides for its funding. These speech courses are generally taught by full-time, degreed college faculty but occasionally by adjunct professors who have an undergraduate degree in some other field and who are gifted communicators. Experienced members of Toastmasters clubs sometimes fill this role. Many people who have developed public speaking skills and have degrees and experience in other disciplines are engaged to teach one or two community college courses on a part-time basis.

Liberal arts colleges are likely to offer a much richer selection of speech courses than are community colleges but are more likely to engage full-time faculty members. In addition to the courses offered at community colleges, they may offer courses in business and professional speaking, rhetorical criticism, parliamentary procedure, speechwriting, theories of persuasion, nonverbal communication, communication and social change, political communication, and skills for briefings and sales presentations. Many colleges encourage participation in intercollegiate forensics. Some of them offer academic credit for enrollment in a forensics workshop that includes debate, oratory, impromptu speaking, oral interpretation, and other performance activities. These colleges may also offer evening and weekend courses—both credit and noncredit—especially if no community college is competing for students.

Universities provide much the same variety of courses as colleges on the undergraduate level but with a somewhat greater variety. In general, universities in the West, the South, and the Midwest have larger, stronger speech communication departments than do those in the East. Many universities attract graduate students to their M.A. and Ph.D. programs, in which they take such advanced courses as communication and culture, persuasion theory, language and social interaction, and various seminars and internships. Many students at the doctoral level are granted teaching assistantships during which they develop instructional skills by teaching classes of first-year students.

The doctoral programs in speech communication, like those throughout the university, are research-oriented, consisting of coursework, independent study, and independent scholarly work leading to a thesis or dissertation. Graduate study at the University of Texas, for example, purposes

> to develop the intellectual breadth and to provide the specialized training necessary to a career in teaching, in research, or in the professions. Emphasis is placed on the knowledge, methods, and skills needed for scholarly teaching, original research and problem solving, intellectual leadership, creative expression, and other modes of achievement in the student's discipline.[1]

Notably missing from its purpose is the preparation of students to excel in their discipline as practitioners. The graduate student in speech should not expect to develop speaking skills or to learn how to make a living on the professional speaking platform.

I knew exactly what I wanted to be . . . an on-air radio personality just like my Uncle Keith. Three weeks after I graduated from high school, I passed the test for my third-class radiotelephone operators license. Several weeks after that, I began working evenings and weekends at radio station WBPZ-AM & FM in Lock Haven, Pennsylvania. That same summer, I enrolled at Lock Haven State College. I remember very clearly my first class, Fundamentals of Speech 101 with Dr. Hazel Ray Ferguson. My life would never be the same.

For the next four years, I worked at the radio station, took more courses in speech and drama, appeared in a few plays, and became the sound and lighting wizard for the college theater. I also learned that you can't make a decent living working in small-town radio, but my interests had shifted to television. They installed a closed-circuit television station on campus. Since there were no formal courses in TV, I designed my own independent study. I also changed my career path to become a college professor so I could teach television, radio, and film and produce instructional television programs. That would require at least a master's degree, so I enrolled in the graduate school of communication at Clarion University of Pennsylvania.

Eighteen months later, I had a M.A. in communication and instructional design and two job offers, one teaching in a college and producing instructional television and the other working for an industrial manufacturing firm producing instructional television. I took the manufacturing job and my career path changed again. After 10 years with two Fortune 500 corporations working in training and development, I started my own consulting and training firm. That led to some professional speaking opportunities. When I joined the National Speakers Association, I met the woman who became my wife, and I refocused my career on strategy and leadership development in health care. Today I am a health-care strategist who works with health-care organizations that want to grow and with health-care leaders who want to get ready for the future. I do this through keynote speeches and learning seminars at health-care conferences and association conventions, by leading health-care leaders through a process of refocusing their organizations, and by writing books and articles on the future of health care.

Little did I know that my first college class, Fundamentals of Speech 101, and a B.A. in speech and drama would lead to a fulfilling, satisfying, and lucrative career as a professional speaker, author, and consultant.

Stephen C. Tweed CSP is a principal in the firm of Tweed Jeffries LLC of Louisville, Kentucky, with his wife Elizabeth Jeffries. They are both speakers, consultants, and authors.

TECHNOLOGY-BASED LEARNING

Technology has sparked a revolutionary change in adult education. A generation ago, no one could have imagined its extent today; nor can anyone today totally envision the shape and extent of technology-driven learning our children and grandchildren will enjoy. Two screens are bringing into peoples' homes the information once available only in books and college classrooms: (1) the television screen and (2) the computer screen. People skilled in public speaking are appearing on both those screens, and people who are developing their communication skills are using what they see and hear to achieve their learning and financial objectives.

Many large universities and consortia of smaller colleges are offering televised courses on public television stations or cable channels. Typically, these courses appear between 1:00 A.M. and 6:00 A.M., with the expectation not of a live viewing audience but of being taped for later viewing. By registering at a sponsoring college, a student may earn academic credit. Viewers who do not want credit may simply learn what is offered, with or without the directed reading and learning activities. Courses of special interest to students of human communication include those on such topics as principles of selling, introduction to marketing, discovering psychology, ethics in the United States, American business today, and English composition.

Persons who like to learn by example can draw on an ever-growing collection of videos and CDs documenting speeches given by prominent speakers. The cable network CNN keeps adding to its archives every minute of tape it has recorded since its founding in 1980. CNN tapes of hundreds of speakers are available through the Public Affairs Video Archives at Purdue University in Indiana. Details are available at C-Span's Web Site WWW.C-Span.org. Supplements to the Allyn & Bacon college text, *Public Speaking: Strategies for Success,* by David Zarefsky, include a videotape of 16 student speeches, "Great Speeches from CNN News," and an "Audio Study Guide to Public Speaking." One commercial source of videotaped speeches is Oryx Press, producer of the CD-ROM "Famous American Speeches: 1850 to the Present," which contains more than 300 historical speeches and about 45 minutes worth of multimedia clips [(800) 279-4663]. Designed for high school classes, this video resource is accompanied by study guides.

COMMUNITY-BASED COURSES

Evening and weekend courses in speech communication are not always sponsored by academic institutions. Libraries, churches, youth organizations, and various charitable groups conduct adult education programs.

Libraries

The Forsyth County Library in Winston-Salem, North Carolina, sponsors a full adult continuing education program to help residents learn new trades, hunt for jobs, and develop their communication skills. Thousands of such library programs function throughout the nation, with more to come as welfare recipients are trained for productive work.

High Schools

The Upper Darby High School in Pennsylvania is typical of the high school district that sponsors an adult evening program. Courses generally run for 10 weeks and are offered 2 or 3 times a year. In addition to the standard public speaking course are subjects that skilled speakers can teach, if they are expert in that subject matter area: gardening, computer skills, investments, art appreciation, boating and seamanship skills, photography, and the like. More often than not, administrators of these evening schools are searching for teachers, providing a marvelous opportunity for persons considering a career as a speaker or trainer to gain experience.

Toastmasters

The primary emphasis in meetings of Toastmasters clubs is the development of public speaking skills, but participation in the club's life also produces increased leadership skills. Clubs of 20 to 30 members, more than half of which are sponsored by corporations or government agencies, gather for one to two hours for highly structured meetings. A brief opening business session, usually run with considerable formality, addresses the club's administrative and housekeeping matters. Many clubs emphasize parliamentary procedure in these sessions. A period called Table Topics follows, giving members the opportunity to give impromptu speeches on assigned topics for one to two minutes each. Finally, several people give prepared speeches, usually of five to seven minutes. Many clubs videotape these speeches so speakers can view their presentations at home. Every element of the meeting is evaluated, including each speaker, who is assigned a personal evaluator.

The world headquarters office of Toastmasters International provides a wide variety of resource materials to satisfy the variety of speaking skill levels and the efficient operation of the clubs. New members begin with a Communication and Leadership Program manual that gives them basic insights about public speaking and encourages them to complete a 10-speech goal that will reward them with the CTM designation—Competent Toastmaster. They may then elect a communication track that leads to the designation Advanced Toastmaster Bronze (ATM-B) or a leadership track that leads to the designation Competent Leader (CL). The club member who is following the communication track may fulfill additional requirements to become an Advanced Toastmaster Silver (ATM-S) and then an Advanced Toastmaster Gold (ATM-G). Persons involved in leadership growth may earn the designation Advanced Leader (AL). Any member may serve a term as president, secretary, sergeant-at-arms, administrative or publicity vice president, or treasurer or may oversee the club's educational program as educational vice president.

Advanced recognition involves giving an additional number of speeches—longer and more challenging ones—or taking on leadership assignments based on advanced manuals. The highest award, Distinguished Toastmaster (DTM), is given to persons who have achieved both the Advanced Toastmaster Gold and the Advanced Leader award. A few highly successful members who have spoken extensively to business and community groups are designated Accredited Speakers. However, even the newest member may earn an award ribbon for being best speaker or best Table Topics speaker of the evening—even for being the best evaluator. An elaborate system of awards helps to form the Toastmaster culture that motivates performance with group recognition. A modest yearly dues covers most of the costs of participation.

Many Toastmasters choose to participate in speaking contests, all of which begin at the club level. The winner of a club contest in speaking, giving table topics, humorous speech, or evaluating may move up to one or more contest levels—division, district, regional, and international.

COMMERCIAL COURSES

Public Seminars

All the major public seminar companies list one-day courses in public speaking, along with such courses as conflict resolution, using the Internet, and customer service. The cost ranges from $99 to $199. SkillPath Seminars offers a typical speech course titled "Speak Up and Stand Out: How to Make Presentations with Confidence, Credibility, and Power." The course covers the following modules:

- Preparation means perfect presentations
- Putting it all together
- Managing pre-presentation jitters and stage fright
- Polishing your delivery
- Using visual aids effectively

- Powerful persuasion techniques
- Continuing to develop and sharpen your speaking skills

The carefully chosen instructors for these courses are highly competent and, almost without exception, deliver an excellent seminar. The expectation for achievement, however, may be set unrealistically high. The course description ends: "Don't you owe it to yourself to add the ability to make effective presentations to your repertoire of career skills? It's easy—and it takes just one day." It strains the imagination to believe that any effective speaker—amateur or professional—developed their expertise in just one day. The probability is even less likely for the 50 to 200 people who fill a hotel room for these seminars, with no opportunity to practice their skills. Another seminar company's brochure even promises that no one will be asked to stand up and say anything. The value of these seminars lies in either being an introduction to public speaking for someone who has no information at all or as a refresher course for the experienced speaker.

Most of these companies offer workbooks, audio albums, and videotapes to augment their seminars or to provide help to people who cannot attend a seminar. They also offer customized on-site training for companies that will provide sufficient time for skill building.

Dale Carnegie Courses

Dale Carnegie is one of America's oldest and most respected providers of training in communication skills. Founded and named after the author of one of the 1930s' most influential books, *How to Win Friends and Influence People,* it sponsors classes in more than 80 countries.

The basic "Dale Carnegie Course" is a human relations course, taught in 12 evenings, designed to raise the participants' self-confidence levels through public speaking and other assignments. An advanced course, "High Impact Presentations," involves 5 to 12 people in a two-day intensive course that majors in public speaking. Students present several five-minute speeches that are videotaped, with two instructors available for on-the-spot coaching. One of the speech assignments is to liven up a dull, written speech students are given; another is a "Meet the Press" exercise. Graduates of the basic course may receive three college credits from the State University of New York or earn 4.2 Continuing Education Units.

The opportunity to be a Dale Carnegie instructor is available to people who have finished the courses and taken enough additional hours to complete the 400 hours required for an instructorship. Most instructors are avocational, continuing to pursue their full-time business or professional careers.

Executive Speaker Training

A number of training companies, most of them local or regional, also offer on-site training in communication skills, but some offer their training to the public as well. The format of their instruction is roughly the same as the Dale Carnegie "High Impact Presentations" course, with intensive on-site seminars for one or two days.

Topics that drive the agenda include: the speaker as a person, analyzing the audience, choosing a topic, doing research, organizing the ideas, finding supporting material, wording the presentation, fine tuning the voice and body skills, rehearsing, and improving the presentation.

When a company engages a speech training company for an on-site seminar, both participant and instructor have one major advantage over the Dale Carnegie or any standard course: the instructor can assess the needs of the participants by interviewing the company's training manager or the participants' supervisors. Knowing the speaker's strengths and weaknesses as a presenter gives the instructor a head start in achieving both the company's and the learner's goals. The trainer may also be able to schedule follow-up sessions to check the learners' developing skills.

Companies engage this kind of training for a number of reasons. One is that they want to increase sales production, much of which occurs in presentations to groups. Another is to achieve greater effectiveness of the oral report giving in meetings. In addition, some companies, especially utilities, send employees to service clubs and senior citizen gatherings to interpret the company's position on rates, service, and deregulation. For yet others, the speech seminar is part of the company's executive training program, preparing midlevel managers for executive positions. Senior executives—CEOs and executive vice presidents—rarely take these courses. Probably because they do not want their authority challenged by their subordinates in an evaluation session, they are more likely to engage an instructor as a private coach if they feel the need for help. Executives of extremely large companies tend to rely on their speech writers for coaching, some of whom are quite competent in coaching delivery factors such as voice, gestures, and especially using a teleprompter. Other executives engage an outside speaking coach.

Professional Speaking Seminars

A growing number of high-profile professional speakers are offering seminars and tapes on how to become a successful professional speaker. Some of them simply tell people to do what the professional speakers did, but others are highly organized, content-rich learning experiences with extremely helpful advice. Some of the titles are

- "Speak and Grow Rich"
- "How to Make $25,000 an Hour without a Gun"

- "How to Get Booked and Make Money Fast as a Professional Speaker"
- "Speaking for a Living"
- "Speak, Consult, Publish Successfully"
- "Specialize or Die"
- "Institute for Speaker & Seminar/Conference Marketing"
- "Discover the Profitable World of Professional Speaking"
- "How to Really Make It as a Professional Speaker"

The general pattern for these offers is to hold a one- to four-day intensive seminar and to provide extensive handouts plus both audio- and videotapes. One of the less expensive seminars, "From Amateur to Pro as a Speaker/Trainer," costs about $300 for a one-day seminar. In addition to advice for breaking into the market is a five-to-eight minute presentation that is critiqued. A two-day seminar by a prominent motivational speaker in a Midwestern city is advertised at about $500.

A two and a half-day seminar, with a structured, year-long program of follow-up phone appointments, costs $1,500. A marketing expert, working with several prominent platform speakers, offers a four-day seminar—10 to 14 hours each day—for $4,000. Another prominent speaker offers a five-day seminar to a small group for $7,250, including workbook, books, tapes, and most meals but with no follow-up promised.

One program without an opening seminar for its participants—the "Million Dollar Speaker Program"—offers a "fully integrated, multimedia system" incorporating not only a large number of tapes but also contact software, samples of marketing materials, and, of course, abundant printed how-to materials. The cost is around $1,500 and includes discount coupons for the Million Dollar Speaking Summits to be offered in subsequent months. Ads for this and other programs appear in *Sharing Ideas*. Announcement of subsequent seminars and programs is mailed to National Speakers Association and American Society for Training and Development members and to lists purchased by the programs' sponsors.

Advice offered to persons who wish to become paid speakers is also available in a number of books listed in Appendix D, some out-of-print but occasionally available in public libraries and through out-of-print book merchants. The most widely read of these books, *Speak and Grow Rich,* by Dottie and Lilly Walters, provides the basis for their "Speak and Grow Rich" seminar, offered frequently in a variety of cities.

Seminars of the National Speakers Association

In addition to these commercially sponsored seminars is an educational program offered several times throughout the year by the National Speakers Association. The NSA has developed one of the richest resources for developing speaking skills at a very high level of professionalism, the International Center for Professional Speaking at its Tempe, Arizona, office. Throughout the year, the center hosts groups of up to 100 who spend two and a half days learning from the speaking industry's top professionals. The cost ranges from $200 to $300, depending on date of registration and membership status. The wide range of topics covered include

- Topic Development and Material Research: How to Identify, Develop and Promote Your Topic to Today's Most Eager Markets
- Marketing Skills for the Professional Speaker: Marketing Strategies That Are Working for Some of NSA's Most Successful Speakers
- Platform Skills for the Professional Speaker
- On the Money: Where to Get It; How to Get It; How to Keep It; How to Keep It Growing
- Humor and Storytelling Skills for the Professional Speaker

- Technology Skills for the Professional Speaker
- Authorship Skills for the Advanced Professional Speaker
- Sales Skills for the Professional Speaker
- Product Development Skills for the Professional Speaker

Each of these workshops is also available in an Audio Learning Resource Package and a Video Learning Resource Package, which include tapes and the program workbook. Some NSA chapters use modules from these packages in their programming, presented by facilitators certified by the NSA. Both the audiotape set and the videotape set are competitively priced.

Many NSA chapters sponsor yearly speakers schools, generally all-day Saturday affairs to which anyone in the area who is interested in developing speaking skills and perhaps a speaking business is invited. Most chapters charge around $100 as a registration fee. A recent school sponsored by the National Capital Speakers Association in Washington, D.C., offered participants information on how to

- Hold your audience
- Create your future
- Make humor work for you
- Master powerful moments on the platform
- Speak from strength
- Translate focus into power
- Avoid the three biggest mistakes
- Script, outline, and prepare without looking canned
- Open with impact and close with direction
- Rechannel stress into energy
- Use body language to underline your message
- Orchestrate attention to produce action

Since many—if not all—of the speakers and breakout session leaders are members of the National Speakers Association, these workshops provide them an opportunity to make presentations to both peers and to emerging speakers. Professional speakers are frequently asked to fill speaking assignments at these chapter workshops.

ACTING CLASSES AND LESSONS

Platform appearances share many elements with stage appearances. While the speaker or trainer does not pretend to be an actor, he or she uses many of the techniques that actors use. The speaker has to be skillful in entering and leaving a space; to optimize posture, movement, and gestures of both face and body; and to employ the various skills of the voice. Unlike actors, speakers use material they themselves have researched and created, but sometimes they quote the words of others. Acting skill helps the speaker to set those quoted words apart, acknowledging that they came from another person but that they are conveying the speaker's ideas or feelings differently than the speaker.

Especially valuable to speakers is training in improvisational acting. Joanne Schlosser of Scottsdale, Arizona, says of her improvisational comedy class, "My movements have become more fluid and natural. My ability to project vocally has increased tremendously . . . Improvisational theater techniques will energize your presentations, keep your audiences actively involved, and drive your message home."[2] Acting classes are widely available through community colleges and theater groups in many cities.

STORYTELLING GROUPS

Perhaps the most powerful rhetorical tool the speaker has is the ability to tell stories. Motivational and personal development speeches depend heavily on stories. Even informational speeches take on a special quality when the presenter can couch abstract or esoteric data in the form of a story. Professional speech writers and coaches of business speakers know that they can prod speeches alive simply by converting expository material into a narrative. The dry as dust doctor will say, "Prior to treating a disease, the physician has to identify the symptoms, determine the etiology, and then arrive at the diagnosis." The doctor who is a skilled storyteller will take a bit longer to say, "A little girl came into my office yesterday and asked, 'How do you know what's wrong with people?' I said to her, 'Well, first of all, I ask, "Where are you hurting?" and then I ask some other questions . . .'" What the storytelling speaker is doing is creating a world in listeners' minds into which they can enter with the whole of their beings. That is why everybody loves stories and why meeting planners pay some of their biggest fees to the speakers who are master storytellers.

Many communities have groups of people who love to tell and swap stories. They are almost always known to the reference or the children's librarian in the public library. The National Storytellers Association, numbering about sixty-five hundred persons, provides a wide variety of gatherings and resources for storytellers at all levels of interest and skill. Each October, more than ten thousand people from throughout the world converge in the now-famous Tennessee town of Jonesborough for a storytelling festival. The group's bimonthly *Storytelling Magazine* contains a variety of articles, stories, announcements of local gatherings, and advertisements for professional storytellers. Information about this organization is in Appendix B.

SPEAKING CIRCLES

A few years ago, Lee Glickstein of San Francisco inaugurated a technique for training in public speaking that involves 8 to 10 people who meet for two and a half hours once a week as a support/learning group. He calls his approach Transformational Speaking, "a new way to communicate based on relaxed, natural, authentic human connections and on accessing your genuine passions." Using his approach, the participants quickly get beyond their fear of speaking and develop a close rapport with audience members. The method draws heavily on psychotherapeutic techniques, emphasizing listening, rapport, eye contact, envisioning, and honest sharing of feelings within the protection of a confidential environment. Speakers who are members of the Ohio Speakers Forum have developed several such circles and attribute much of their financial success on the platform to these circles.

COACHING

Many speakers rely on the advice of a sympathetic spouse or close friend who, lacking objectivity, may be too easy or too hard on the speaker or may miss the point altogether. However, many effective speakers swear by the influence of a spouse or partner whose perceptiveness and mentoring skill constitutes an important dimension of the speaker's success.

Just as golfers and singers—even at the peak of their careers—hire coaches, so also do speakers in increasing numbers. Two factors contribute to this growth: (1) the maturation of the speaking profession—now well into its third decade of life as an organized force in society and the business world—and (2) the increasing competitiveness of speaking as a business. Business and association executives and university personnel who choose speakers have a wider variety to choose from than ever. In the mature phase of any business, there is an inevitable shakeout of weaker businesses. Full-time professional speakers who feel the competitive heat engage coaches to help them compete successfully.

Speaking coaches may be found in the ranks of college professors, active or retired. Many of them offer wisdom born of an excellent graduate degree and many years of helping young speakers perform at their best. They have coached debate teams, mentored students for oratorical and other forensic contests, directed plays, and finely honed their own mentoring skills. Some professional speakers, slowing down on their way to retirement, may take on a younger colleague in a mentoring relationship with or without an hourly fee. Owners of speakers bureaus occasionally offer coaching services based on many years of hearing a wide variety of subjects and styles and on keen knowledge of the demands of the marketplace. Many NSA chapters offer a mentoring program to enable experienced speakers to help emerging ones. A few NSA members have built an important part of their business as coaches for business and professional speakers—among them Max Dixon, Patricia Ball, Mary Beth Roach, Robert Gedaliah, and me. Speakers who invest in a competent professional coach testify that the help they receive is the most cost-effective relationship they have ever entered into.

VIDEO WATCHING

Listening to first-rate speakers on a regular basis is one of the most important activities a budding speaker can engage in. Using satellite technology, viewers of The Peoples Network (TPN) can receive several hours each evening of presentations by dozens of well-known speakers, all of whom convey positive motivational messages. Some of the biggest names in the professional speaking industry provide tapes of their platform presentations or present talks customized for this format.

BOOKS AND PERIODICALS

Just as the most important position in any speech is the conclusion, so also do books and magazines occupy the final section of this chapter on learning and teaching. Books on public speaking in its various dimensions occupy shelves in every public library in the land. There is hardly a bookstore that does not carry at least a few books on the subject; the larger ones may devote many feet of shelf space to books on speaking. Some excellent reading is available in both popular and scholarly periodicals on speech communication. Good reading has inaugurated many a career and carried many a speaker to great heights. Profitable reading matter is not hard to find, but absorbing the insights of what you read and putting them into practice is the challenge. What is absolutely certain is that an ongoing habit of reading about this fascinating subject is indispensable to every speaker's success.

The nation's most successful speakers are the first to advise the "wannabes" who ask for advice on starting a speaking business to do whatever it takes to keep growing, learning, and developing. They know better than anyone that the price to be paid for success—however measured—is constant learning. Fortunately, the opportunities to grow as a speaker have never been greater.

NOTES

1. The University of Texas at Austin, *The Graduate Catalog,* 1995–1997, p. 2.

2. Joanne Schlosser, "Energize Your Training Sessions with Improvisational Theater Techniques," *Professional Speaker*, November 1996, p. 28.

6 Celebrity Speakers

Celebrity speakers make their living by doing the things that made them celebrities, or they live on their royalties and investments. They are television news anchors, retired astronauts, business management superstars, actors, best-selling authors, famous athletes, former political officeholders, victims or perpetrators of high-profile crimes, victorious military officers, and the like. They add whatever speaking fees they earn to already substantial incomes—or they replace those incomes with speaking fees when they move out of their celebrity jobs.

This book devotes its shortest chapter to celebrity speakers because they are by far the smallest segment of the speaking business. They are an important part of it, however, for two reasons: (1) their presence on the platform constantly calls attention to the importance of speaking in the world of business and community life, and (2) they are competitors of the vastly larger number of persons who fill the country's speaking engagements. This book can't provide guidance to becoming a celebrity, but it can briefly document the role of celebrities in the speaking business.

Celebrity speaking is, of course, not a new occupation. Charles Dickens, Mark Twain, P. T. Barnum, Ralph Waldo Emerson, and William Jennings Bryan are sometimes cited as early examples of professional speakers, but they were really celebrity speakers. Like today's avocational and full-time speakers, however, their income came from diverse sources. Dickens, Twain, and Emerson were primarily writers, and Barnum kept busy running his circus. Bryan was a distinguished attorney, former United States Secretary of State under President Wilson, and three times a candidate for president of the United States. The embryo of what has become a huge supporting business for professional speakers also arose in the form of a company called the Redpath Bureau in Boston that arranged for the bookings of those early speakers on the Chautauqua Circuit and elsewhere. This book's final chapter will trace the development of this early support structure into the enormous, complex system of companies and individuals that has grown around the speaking business.

Along with the status of celebrity come extremely high speaking fees. Our television-dominated culture pays huge amounts of money to people who entertain by singing and playing, who engage in sports, or who communicate the news winsomely. Audiences want to see and hear those glamorous figures, as well as the people who make the news and write the books on the *New York Times* best-sellers list. They value people who are mentioned in the gossip columns or who occupy positions of power in business or government. They are fascinated by people whose columns predict the future and artists who can talk intelligently about their work in music, painting, the theater, or poetry. The demand for personal appearances drives up celebrities' speaking fees well beyond those of most business speakers.

A speaking date by ex-President George Bush at a 1993 Amway convention for $100,000 made news throughout the country, but Bill Cosby raised his speaking fee to that amount shortly thereafter. A recent issue of *Meetings & Conventions* reported that Phyllis George, former Miss America, "former First Lady of Kentucky and sportscaster," charges $12,500 and up for speaking on "inspirational, motivational, humorous, arts and crafts" topics. In the same issue, Roger Staubach, formerly a football star and now a commercial real estate investor, charges $10,000 in the Dallas, Texas, area and $13,000 outside Dallas.[1] Meeting planners for large corporations, associations, and college lecture committees pay $75,000 and up for first-rank celebrity speakers.

Bureau owners recently revealed the single engagement fees of several celebrities, some of which are commissionable to bureaus and some that constitute the net income to the celebrity. These fees do not include travel—usually first-class air—and other out-of-pocket expenses:

- Olympia Dukakis, actress: $17,500
- Ruth Westheimer, sex therapist and author: $12,000
- Jerry Brown, ex-governor of California and U.S. presidential candidate: $9,500
- Magic Johnson, athlete: $50,000
- James Redfield, best-selling author: $17,500
- Marian Wright Edelman, advocate for children: $13,800
- Felicia Rashad, actress: $20,000
- Coretta Scott King, widow of Dr. Martin Luther King, Jr.: $13,800
- Louis Rukeyser, economic commentator: $40,000
- Deepak Chopra, physician and author: $25,000[2]

Like all speakers' fees, celebrities' fees are determined by the law of supply and demand. Superstars like Magic Johnson, whose total income from team sports and endorsements is phenomenal, may even set their fees at a high level to reduce the demand. Other extremely high-profile celebrities who don't like to speak, don't need the money, and have nothing to say anyway have been known to set such high speaking fees that they do not have to refuse requests.

The messages celebrity speakers bring is as wide as the experiences that brought them to the platform. People in political life may speak about the values that make the United States great and urge greater participation in solving its problems. Actors may share experiences that have made their lives interesting, or they may espouse some cause like the environment or AIDS research. Athletes weave their experiences on the playing field with lessons on leadership, teamwork, or communication skills. Journalists may offer their opinions on societal or political trends they are observing. While audiences value the messages of these speakers, the reality of celebrity speaking is that they are frequently booked to ensure a large attendance at a meeting.

SPOKESPERSONS

Spokespersons are celebrities who are paid by a corporation or are engaged as volunteers by a nonprofit organization to represent that group. The public thinks of spokespersons primarily as television performers. Jim Palmer speaks for The Money Store, June Allyson for Depends, Betty White for US Healthcare. However, some spokespersons also appear on speaking platforms, usually to address a national convention of their sponsor's employees or an audience that organization wants to impress with its interest or generosity.

QUASI-CELEBRITIES

Some people become widely known not because they themselves are outstanding actors, writers, Olympic medal winners, or achievers of some great feat but because they are connected with persons who are celebrities. An example is Jeff Feiger, the attorney whose representation of Dr. Jack Kevorkian, dubbed by the press as the Death Doctor, has opened the door to many profitable speaking engagements at $5,750 each. Johnnie Cochran, Marcia Clark, Christopher Darden, and Robert

Shapiro, attorneys who figured prominently in the 1995 murder trial of O. J. Simpson, assumed celebrity status after the trial and became popular, well-paid speakers.

Audiences will always crave celebrities for their meetings, and celebrities will always be available for large fees. One cannot understand the speaking business without taking them into account as an important factor. But people who want to enter the speaking business need to understand that they do not need to be celebrities to be successful, well-paid speakers.

NOTES

1. Marc Boisclair, "Big Mouths," *Meetings & Conventions*, November 1994, pp. 9–12.
2. Ibid. Reprinted with permission of MEETINGS & CONVENTIONS magazine, November 1994 © by Cahners Publishing, Reed Elsevier Inc.

7 Avocational Speakers

So you're thinking about becoming a professional speaker? Can't wait to visit all those luxurious places and sleep in fancy hotels while becoming a household name? Let me give you a piece of advice; don't quit your day job.

Most of those places turn out to be Fargo, North Dakota, Menopause, Nebraska, or Piscataway, New Jersey, with hotels named The Inn At Exit 9 or Big Betty's Hideaway, and the only household in which you become a name is your own.

During my years of professional speaking, I have also been a successful salesperson. This gave me the opportunity to pick and choose my speaking engagements. Which, by the way, is the best reason for remaining a part-time speaker. You can decline any offer for any reason and still make your mortgage payment.

I began my career as a Dale Carnegie course instructor. All I had to do was show up and speak. The hard work of marketing and selling was done before I opened my mouth. I always had a full house. Most full-time speakers can't make that claim. After five years of Dale Carnegie, I had had enough. Speaking in the same hotel with the same material for five years led me to believe I could do better, make more money, and have more fun. I was partly right.

Although I got paid for every speech delivered, I never really knew what a professional speaker was until

I attended my first National Speakers Association convention in 1984. The amount of changes that have occurred since then are staggering. But through it all certain constants remain: (1) I am still a salesperson first and a professional speaker second, (2) 25 percent of my income is from speaking, (3) my topic after all these years is still sales, and (4) my audiences never exceed 40 people. I do, however, limit my speaking to only three markets, do charge considerably more than when I started, and have upgraded my brochure to be more commensurate with my fee.

I feel comfortable knowing that each call to a prospective meeting planner is not a do-or-die situation, and if all the people I talk to in a week say no, I can still make my mortgage payment.

Geoffrey D. Riddle is president of Innocom International, a sales training firm in Scottsdale, Arizona.

SOME DEFINITIONS

Celebrity speakers, the first category of people who earn money on the platform, should be clearly understood through the material in Chapter 6. Before attempting to define avocational speaking, however, it is important to understand the people who occupy the third category, full-time business speakers, to be discussed at greater length in the next chapter.

Full-time business speakers generally combine their speaking with training, consulting, and product sales to earn their entire income. Many of them make relatively high incomes, although their speaking fees are rarely comparable to celebrity fees. Full-time business speakers operate primarily on the platform and in corporate training rooms, addressing corporation and association audiences all over the country and, increasingly, throughout the world. Many also consult and sell informational products. They are sophisticated marketers who have established themselves as authorities in one or more of a variety of fields. The busiest ones charge $2,000 to $5,000 per speech or training assignment, although some speak for less and others for more.

An avocational speaker, on the other hand, has a full-time job or profession to which speaking for fees is added income. That job may be closely related to speaking—like training or consulting—or very different, like practicing law or dentistry, managing a company, or selling real estate.

Avocational speakers usually speak and train on the topic that gives them their livelihood, although sometimes they speak on a totally different topic about which they have developed information and expertise. They are also called *second-income speakers*—college professors, management con sultants, financial writers, corporate managers, university administrators, authors, and experts of various kinds. Most function out of their own offices, some are involved with the NSA, and others are unconnected to any group of speakers. When they appear before groups within their own industries, they are called *industry speakers*. Many avocational speakers—especially on topics of general interest, such as success, self-esteem, and coping with difficult people—appear in a wide variety of venues, including business groups, trade and professional associations, and college campuses. It is not uncommon for an avocational speaker to earn more money on the platform than on the day job.

Avocational speaking is not an easily recognizable category in the National Speakers Association or in the increasing number of books and tapes designed to help people enter the business of paid speaking. The help offered to beginning speakers in these books and tapes, and the major speeches and breakout sessions at NSA conventions and chapter meetings, advise listeners on how they can earn an outstanding income as full-time platform speakers. While no figures are kept, people familiar with the makeup of the NSA membership estimate that a very large number are avocational speakers and plan to remain in that category.

Another place avocational speakers develop their skills and find support is in Toastmasters clubs. While these clubs by their very nature offer limited guidance to speakers who may wish to profit financially from their speaking skills, many members do profit from their Toastmasters experience by earning money as avocational speakers. Most Toastmasters who speak to community audiences probably do so on a *pro bono* basis, but many speak for fees as avocational income or as a step toward full-time speaking.

There is one other category of speaker who doesn't quite fit the list. It is the *never-been-paid speaker* or the *tired-of-doing-freebies speaker.* If you are one of those, you know the symptoms. You have won any number of Toastmasters contests, spoken at any number of Rotary meetings, addressed any number of in-service days for teachers or health-care professionals—and have done so gladly. But no one has ever put a $100 bill in your hand as you walked to your car after a speaking engagement or enclosed a check in the thank-you letter. You may have developed into a speaker with the skill that rivals a paid speaker but haven't learned—or tried—to ask for a fee or to market yourself in a businesslike way.

WHY PEOPLE CHOOSE AVOCATIONAL SPEAKING

Why do people choose to be avocational speakers? One reason is that they have developed a relatively secure income from their primary job and they are reluctant to risk trying to earn their living on the platform, even if they are unhappy in their work. Perhaps even more important is that they genuinely like what they are doing, convinced that it is what they are supposed to be doing with their lives; their primary occupation is for them a calling. Still others have looked at the lifestyle of full-time speakers, frequently involving long absences from home and unpredictable income, and have decided that the stability of a good job and of spending time with their families is more important than any amount of money that may await them on the speaking platform.

TOPICS FOR AVOCATIONAL SPEAKERS

Avocational speakers speak on many of the same topics as full-time, professional speakers, but they may address topics a full-time speaker would not find cost-effective. Full-time business speakers have to find clients that pay substantial fees in the interest of increasing their productivity with fresh information or motivational power. Avocational speakers can and do fill these engagements, but they can also address smaller and more specialized audiences. A tax attorney can address a local association of accountants on the implications of a proposed real estate tax increase, earning $100 or $200 but also gaining valuable exposure to people who may retain his professional services at a later date. A regional consortium of garden clubs might pay a florist who has developed a popular and entertaining talk on the growing of orchids. These are assignments that no full-time professional speaker can usually afford to take.

Persons earning a living at a day job are experts on something—perhaps in a variety of areas. You have gained experience or a body of knowledge that may be clearly useful to others. What you know may make you a genuine expert—even a world-class authority. Or you may be proficient in an area that is totally unrelated to your work. Perhaps you have some valuable information about a subject that fascinates you, along with the curiosity to learn more. It could well lead to a platform speech that deserves a fee. Your first task as an avocational speaker is to identify some area of knowledge, some skill, or some insight on life that the audience is eager enough to pay for and that you know enough to talk about with authority.

Note which task is first: the willingness of the audience to pay for your expertise and speaking skill. If your goal is to enjoy some profit from your speaking, you must choose a topic with the possibility of earning money. You may present to Toastmasters or an evening college speech class a wonderful talk on finding your ancestors or housebreaking puppies, but if you are serious about launching a speaking business, you will choose topics with profit potential. If you have been speaking to service clubs for no money, you will need to examine whether your topic has genuinely commercial possibilities. What you are searching for is an intersection between what you are qualified to share and what people will pay to hear.

Topics for General Audiences

What interests today's audiences ranges from the very general to the highly specific. Everyone wants to know how to get along with family and friends, to make and manage money more skillfully, to stay well, to manage time efficiently, and to deal with the stresses of a changing world. You can't go wrong with any of these topics. One of the topics most frequently listed by meeting planners is success. Anyone who has achieved success, however measured, is a candidate to speak about it. When achievement rises out of failure, a personal tragedy, or a physical handicap, audiences are ready to respond. You can speak on these topics at any service club, association meeting, employee club, senior adult gathering, or cruise.

Work-Related Topics

People in a work environment share these general concerns with the general population but they have additional needs. People in the workplace need to know how to deal with customers, to work in teams, to speak and write clearly, to live and work in a diverse workforce, and to maintain high self-esteem in a competitive environment.

At a recent meeting of the International Group of Agencies and Bureaus, the trade association for speakers bureaus, these topics were listed as being in greatest demand:

- Change
- Customer service
- Global opportunities
- Computers and technology
- Future strategies
- Quality
- Productivity/performance
- Business and the economy
- Diversity
- Health and fitness
- Management skills
- Managing stress

Those in your audiences who are supervisors not only share the same needs as the general population and those of the workplace but also need additional help. They have responsibility for building successful teams, exercising leadership, interviewing and hiring the right people, writing performance appraisals, and interpreting complex government regulations.

A glance through a recent catalog of SkillPath Seminars, a large public seminar company, lists the following topics for people in management:

- Successful project management skills
- Conflict resolution and confrontation management
- Fundamentals of finance and accounting for nonfinancial managers
- Managing multiple projects, objectives, and deadlines
- Conflict management skills for women
- The indispensable assistant
- Enlightened leadership: bridge the gap between managing and leading
- Management skills for new supervisors
- Coaching and teambuilding skills for managers and supervisors

During one calendar year, the company may offer each one of these topics hundreds of times, in nearly every state in the union. This highly successful company has fine-tuned its offerings to the point that any one of these topics is guaranteed to draw a large number of people.

Highly Specialized Topics

The more narrowly focused occupations and professions are, the more likely they are to engage speakers who can tackle highly specialized topics.

People in sales or sales management, for example, have a different set of needs from general business managers. They need to know about partnering, making cold calls, relationship selling, and personality characteristics of prospects. Certified Public Accountants need someone to help them keep up with the ever-changing IRS regulations. Neurosurgeons, waste management specialists, federal procurement officers, forensic psychologists, retail store managers, and a thousand other specialized groups value information on topics that go beyond their present knowledge and skill level. They gather in their associations or companies to hear their peers or paid speakers qualified to address them on these subjects. Many of the speakers they engage are avocational speakers.

The reality of today's changing economy, with increased specialization in its every facet, ensures unending new opportunities for speaking and training.

Topics for College Audiences

College and university students possess unique needs. Their age and culture predispose them to speakers who understand them and speak their language. While the college faculty generally does an excellent job of addressing student concerns through the curriculum, their directors of residence halls and student activities committees spend large amounts of money to bring guest speakers to their campuses. Examples of such speakers include Bradley Richardson, the author of *Jobsmarts for Twentysomethings,* who speaks to graduating seniors on how to find good jobs. Rosalyn Meadow, a psychologist and sex therapist in private practice, speaks on "Good Girls Don't Eat Dessert," about women with diagnosed eating disorders but also about other women whose fear of being fat is tied in with issues of identity, self-esteem, career goals, and sexual behavior. William Kane, an attorney by training and now an English professor at Boston College, speaks on "The Art of Kissing," an entertaining consideration of this alternative form of intimacy in the age of AIDS. All these speakers are avocational speakers. A topic in constant demand by college audiences is how to find a job after graduation. A speaker who treats this topic authoritatively, practically, and entertainingly can't go wrong.

The Entertainment Dimension

Nearly every audience has the need to smile and laugh. Some audiences that gather for a banquet or in a final session after some intense learning want simply to be entertained, and they will hire a humorist. Other audiences, gathered for instruction or inspiration, respond positively to incidental humor—especially if it is related to the topic or to their work. The audience's need for entertainment may also be satisfied with some well-told stories or a phrase here or there that conveys a light touch on an otherwise serious subject. An entertainment factor is increasingly becoming a standard expectation for almost any speech. Indeed, most operators of speakers bureaus know that one of the primary determinants of a speaker's fee is the speech's entertainment dimension.

There is some truth to the story often told among speakers about the beginner who asked Bill Gove, one of the NSA's founders, "Do you have to be funny to be a professional speaker?" The answer: "Only if you want to get paid."

Your Own Topics

Using Your Expertise

If you speak on a specialized topic for specialized audiences, your topic choices are made for you. You may be an attorney who speaks most profitably to executives of retirement communities on contracts with residents, a physician who addresses insurance managers on the costs of in-patient care, a kitchen and bath designer who speaks to building contractors: the possibilities are endless.

Like many other speakers, I came into this career through the back door, in my case by developing skills as a detective and then being asked to teach those skills to others. I learned that as I gained knowledge and experience as an investigator, many people asked me to share that knowledge by speaking at our local and national investigator conferences.

As new people within the business heard me speak, my investigation business grew and clients from related fields like paralegals, insurance adjusters, and attorneys—people who could ultimately be clients as well as audiences—asked me to speak at their meetings and conferences as well.

Through a balance of managing a business, consulting on cases with clients, and speaking on new trends in crime and fraud, I find that I have the best of both worlds, doing and teaching, both of which bring referrals and provide a growing income.

One advantage of speaking as a second career is that working in the field provides a host of new speaking material. Almost all the investigations that I am involved in have some new wrinkle or give me a new story that I can share with my audiences who relate them to their own personal business problems.

The interesting nature of my work, combined with the public's fascination with detectives, brings many opportunities for publicity and media exposure. With all the media attention, I had to write a book. Starting with a manual I had written for my investigators, I took some time out in the Bahamas to put together a book that told people how to *Check It Out. I* couldn't find a publisher because they didn't believe that a private investigator could write, so I created my own publishing company, Cloak and Data Press, and self-published my book. Soon I was selling books through the media exposure and my seminars, and then a national publisher picked up my book. *Check It Out* has been on the market now for four years and is selling better today than its first year of publication.

Today I find myself with not two but three careers—consulting, speaking, and writing. I'm looking forward to a smooth, slow transition toward semi-retirement where I do less pounding the pavement and a little more speaking (I found a whole new audience in mystery writers—sweet little old ladies bent on learning the newest techniques in death and destruction). For me, the combination of speaking, making new friends through personal contacts, and travel opportunities makes me feel that I truly have the best of all worlds.

Edmund J. Pankau is president of Pankau Consulting, Houston, Texas, Investigative and Security Consultants.

Becoming an Expert

On what topic can you *become* an expert? You may discover a profitable avocational speaking business by targeting an area of need about which you know relatively little and have little experience. Many speakers have set out to learn nearly everything there is to learn about a topic they knew would be in demand and gone on to experience considerable success. While it can be done, the risks in taking this approach should be obvious. For one thing, by establishing your expertise solely by reading and observing, you will lack the authority, depth, and personal touch that first-person stories bring to any presentation. Also, you may find yourself out of your depth in a question-and-answer session that follows your talk.

One method to assess the viability of popular topics for general audiences may be found in a survey of the talks announced in the community activities section of your local newspaper. Or spend some time in the periodicals section of your local library to see what subjects people are reading about. When you are attracted to one of them, do some creative thinking to discern how you can put a spin on one that will make it your very own. Some speech topics noted in a recent weekly suburban community newspaper include:

- Options for your aging parents
- How managed care will affect your family
- Will you ever drive an electric car?
- When the Internet comes to your house
- The bank of the future
- Painless dentistry—fact or fiction?
- Food supplements for better health
- How to control the TV monster
- Commodities trading—delight or danger?

Another way to discover the topics of interest to audiences in your community is to phone the presidents of local clubs whose programs feature speakers: the Rotary Club, the Business and Professional Women's Club, the American Association of Retired Persons. Ask them for a rundown on topics they have recently heard. In addition, query them on topics they would like to offer to their group. The following list, similar to the one above, came from some club presidents contacted by phone.

- How to stay up in a down world
- Ten commandments of money management
- Don't be a crime victim
- Eat and drink your way to better health
- Stretching your retirement income
- Enrich your business through creative problem solving
- Buying and selling your home in today's economy

The first time I got paid for a speech was for a women's organization in my community that asked me to speak. They offered to pay me $50. At that time I was trying to grow my business promoting health and nutrition, and I thought it was a good way to promote what I was doing, so I said sure! Then after doing it several times I thought, "Oh, I like this!" Then it began to feel like a calling. Someone who knew me personally knew that I had my own business and they wanted me to share what I knew about health and wellness. It was really for the topic, rather than for me. At the time the money was great! It was mostly to help me promote my business, and it was a great way to pass out 200 business cards at once.

Janice L. Krouskop is principal of DBA: Recipes for Personal Success in Pittsburgh, Pennsylvania.

THE PROSPECTS FOR AVOCATIONAL SPEAKING

Who is doing avocational speaking? Who is hiring avocational speakers? What kinds of fees are they getting? A recent survey conducted by Speaker Services, a Philadelphia-area speakers bureau that also offers consulting services for beginning speakers, produced these examples:

- Susan, an administrative assistant, spoke to a chapter of Professional Secretaries International on interpersonal communication skills for $100.
- Tom, a chemical engineer, spoke on time management for a department store that sponsored a series of adult education programs as one of their marketing tools. He earned $50.
- Janet, an attorney, spoke to a regional meeting of the Association of School Business Officials on protecting the

schools from lawsuits around issues of hiring and firing employees. She received a check for $250.

- Barry, a Toastmaster who earns his living in the computer business, did a half-day seminar on presentation skills for a local chapter of the National Management Association. He received $375.
- Delores, a retired U.S. Postal Service manager, made a presentation on customer service in the After-Hours Lifelong Learning Program of a medium-size retail store chain. She took home $200.
- Terry, a professional credit counselor, spoke to a women's club on how to get out of debt and live on a cash basis. She earned $100.

While one or two of these topics require a college education, most of them could have been—and were—developed by people who simply had some experience and the skills to craft and practice a good speech.

STARTING AN AVOCATIONAL SPEAKING BUSINESS

Shall I Call a Speakers Bureau?

You may have heard about the speakers bureaus that book speakers with corporations, associations, and colleges. Signing up with such an organization sounds like an excellent way to begin to enter the speaking business. It is not.

A speakers bureau does broker a deal between speaker and meeting planner but it is not a neutral broker; it works for the meeting planner—an association executive, a company employee charged with planning a convention, or a college Speakers Forum committee. The speakers bureau helps the meeting planner simplify the job by narrowing the choice of speakers, reducing the speaker selection time, ensuring the quality of the speaker chosen, and facilitating the logistics—contracts, travel arrangements, equipment requirements, etc. It draws on its database, personal experience, and sensitivity to the client's needs to find a speaker who can achieve the meeting planner's goal at a price within the planner's budget—all at no cost to the hiring organization. In return for receiving a booking, the speaker pays the bureau a percentage of the fee, usually 25 percent.

It has no interest in working with beginners, because emerging speakers just do not provide the income for the bureau to justify the amount of work it must do to secure the booking. If the speaking fee is $500, the bureau's 25 percent commission, $125, is not likely to cover the bureau's overhead and profit requirements. Bureaus, therefore, don't usually book speakers who charge less than $1,000 per contract. Bureaus also require that the speaker provide the kind of supporting materials that emerging speakers usually don't have—brochures, letters of commendation, pictures, tapes, and news releases.

An even more important reason not to present yourself to a speakers bureau if you are a beginning speaker is that the bureau must assure the meeting planner that the speaker will provide a top level of performance. The bureau's stock in trade is the trust of its clients. It can't provide a guarantee of excellence by offering a client a speaker who is a low-price, unknown quantity. Nearly every bureau, with the exception of those that handle only celebrities, book avocational speakers frequently and with profit, both to themselves and the speaker. But the avocational speakers they book have excellent track records. When you get the reputation of being an outstanding speaker and are earning some serious money—and you have developed some excellent marketing material—both you and a bureau will enjoy working together for your mutual benefit.

Steps to an Avocational Speaking Business

Put Yourself in Perspective

Avocational speaking is midway between speaking for pleasure and speaking for a living. It is more than a hobby and less than an occupation. It is also a business enterprise that requires a high degree of commitment and a great deal of hard work. But it provides a level of personal satisfaction that is difficult to find in any other way. If you love to speak about a topic that is important to you and can discipline yourself to a long-range marketing strategy, you can reap rich rewards. Like others before you, you may keep your day job and have an avocational speaking career too.

If you wish to develop your avocational speaking business into a full-time occupation, you need to be aware of some realities. One is that, except for humorists, ex-celebrities, and a few others, there are few purely "full-time speakers" on today's platforms. Practically all the speakers making a living on the platform live on the income from at least two of four income streams: (1) speaking, (2) training, (3) consulting, and (4) product sales, including books they write and tapes they produce. Many speakers live on a combination of all four. Some have even expanded their basic business by employing a staff of trainers or consultants. You therefore need to gear up for a business characterized by diversity of income—much of it unpredictable.

Another reality is that the likelihood of a smooth transition into a career on the platform is conditioned by the nature of your day job. If you are a corporate or government employee, a busy teacher, a homemaker with small children, a professional person with a successful practice, the owner of a small business with employees who report directly to you, or anyone else with a demanding schedule, the transition is extremely difficult. On the other hand, if you are an independent trainer, a consultant with your own office, or a business owner with a good income and a schedule you can control, it is not such a big jump to becoming a profitable avocational speaker.

Your age, gender, and ethnicity may also be important considerations in evaluating the possibilities of a speaking career. Fortunately, speakers come from all age groups, both genders, all ethnic populations, and from among the ranks of the disabled. While any of these factors may make you less attractive to some audiences, you may be all the more attractive to others. A recent young college graduate, for example, is not able to draw from a rich background of management experience to address an audience of senior executives. That same person, however, may speak with keen insight to that group or another on marketing to Generation X. A young speaker may carry greater credibility on that topic than a 57-year-old marketing middle manager, no matter how experienced. An African American or Hispanic American speaker who can speak on customer service or employee relations may gain access to an audience of human resource directors with a talk on empowering a racially and culturally diverse employee force because the speaker knows from the inside what it is like to work as a minority employee. And who is better qualified to speak on overcoming disabilities than the speaker whose accident placed that speaker in a wheelchair? Or who can better speak on enriching the retirement years than a retiree who is doing exactly that?

A final consideration is that speaking is an ego-driven business. No one stays at it very long, or makes much money at it, who does not possess an unusually high level of self-esteem. The successful speaker, however success is measured, keeps at it out of a sense that being on the platform is just about the most important place in the world and the audience the most important people in the world. Speakers who are successful love being at the center of attention, love applause, love the high that comes with speaker-audience chemistry.

Adopt Clear Goals

However modest or ambitious are the goals in your head, they need at least to be clear and they need to be written down. If you are ambivalent about starting a speaking business—an understandable feeling—you may wish to experiment with the idea for a few months. Or simply adopt a modest goal, like getting one speaking engagement. If you achieve one, you can achieve two, perhaps three. If you use speaking as a marketing tool for your business or profession, aim for one referral, one new client, one product sold. If you aim to earn money as a speaker, shoot for your first $100 fee.

Remember that overarching all these goals is a quest for becoming recognized as an interesting, well-informed speaker who can be counted on to deliver what is promised. The wider and stronger that recognition, the more successful your speaking career will become. Warren Greshes, a highly successful motivational speaker from New York, reminded listeners in "Voices of Experience," an audiotape sent monthly to NSA members, that "your first goal is not money, but reputation."

Optimize Your Speaking Skills

You learned in Chapter 5 about the numerous opportunities to develop your platform skills. Take one opportunity, and then another and another. Your concern to be your very best stands right at the beginning of the process of seeking engagements and continues until the day you die or you decide never to speak in public again. No marketing techniques can take the place of sheer excellence in advancing your speaking career.

Start Where You Are

If you have ever signed on to a multilevel sales enterprise such as Amway, Shaklee, or Herbalife, you learned at your first meeting that the road to success begins by letting your relatives, friends, coworkers, and neighbors know what you are selling. The path to receiving speaking fees begins with developing a list of every speaker-inviting group known to you and the people closest to you. The experience and exposure you will gain in front of those groups is the indispensable first step to becoming an avocational speaker.

Even if you are a world-class expert on a highly specialized topic, begin with service clubs, using an adaptation of your topic for a general audience, or speak on a topic of general interest to gain the experience. Ask your friends, neighbors, and relatives if they belong to a Rotary, Kiwanis, Lions, Optimist, Sertoma, Exchange, or other service club. Ask them whom they know who belongs to a business and professional women's club, a group of retired persons, a small trade association, or a Chamber of Commerce. Nearly every one of these groups has a voracious appetite for speakers and will be glad to hear about you. Develop a simple database of these clubs, adding whatever information you can garner about their officers with addresses and phone numbers, meeting dates and places. In some cases your friends will be willing to propose your name as a speaker; in others, they will provide the name of the program chair whom you can call directly. Set a realistic date for your friend or yourself to begin making the contacts. Appendix F contains a list of the kinds of organizations that engage unpaid speakers.

When you have spoken free of charge many times to service clubs and small trade associations, you can begin thinking about charging a fee to the groups that have a budget item for speakers. In your pre- and postmeeting conversations with club officers, ask if they ever pay speakers and under what circumstances. Add that information to your database.

I was sitting at my kitchen table when I got a call from a woman who wanted me to speak at a luncheon in Waterbury, Connecticut, for the Connecticut Life Underwriters Association. I believe she got my name because I had done a gratis talk at some other association. I was elated. I agreed. I was filling in for some other speaker who had canceled. I was given an honorarium of $150. I had given about a dozen speeches at no charge. One of them was for an insurance organization and one of those people gave her my name.

Joseph Oddie is principal of the Oddie Group, a firm that teaches customer-oriented sales techniques in Meriden, Connecticut.

Raise Your Assertiveness Index

List making and date setting are the danger points for many persons who believe they would like to be paid speakers. While some may plunge wholeheartedly into this task, many people begin to get cold feet at this point. If you are one of them, take note of two barriers that raise themselves—both of them in your perceptions—of the people whose help you seek and of the club's decision makers.

Many people feel that they don't want to take advantage of their friends or relatives to get speaking leads. If that is a hang-up for you, you need to ponder seriously whether you are cut out for a career in speaking—at any level of activity or income. A professional speaker—avocational or full-time—is by definition an unabashed self-promoter. Shyness will not get you very far as a speaker. With no exceptions, the person who develops a speaking business has to believe deep down and communicate to others an attitude that says, "I have something of tremendous importance to say and I am really good at saying it on a platform." You do not need to be arrogant or boastful, but you do need to believe strongly in yourself and what you feel you are called to speak about. If you have those qualities, you have probably already communicated them to your friends, neighbors, and relatives—who will be delighted to help you fulfill your dream. Using these contacts will dramatically reduce the time needed to get started.

Beginning speakers also misperceive the role of meeting planners. The vice president of programs for a service club or trade association has a tough job finding good speakers—especially free ones. Believe it or not, they are not eager to discourage you or chase you away. They really want to know who you are and what you can do for their groups. If your offer to speak is not warmly received, remember that the group may have recently heard a presentation on your topic or that the person you are talking to may have a personal hang-up about your subject. Remember also that someone else will hold that club office in due time and that you can try again. Draw on your reservoir of self-confidence to accept rejection, saying to yourself, "They don't know what they're missing!" and move on to the next one.

The reality is that if you are starting out with dreams about a successful speaking business but don't take action to get in front of your first couple of local groups, you will never get a paid engagement with the regional homebuilders' association or the state real estate board. You will certainly not get booked with General Motors or Microsoft. Hanging out a sign that says **SPEAKER** and waiting for people to call you doesn't work.

Your assertiveness index is also important to your audiences. Whatever your topic, you need to engage your audience for a finite period of time with a sense that your message is the most important thing in the world for them to understand or to feel. Audiences are smart and sensitive—more than many speakers realize. They need to experience you as an outgoing person with a strong belief in yourself, embracing them, inviting them to enter into something you feel to be enormously important. When they do, they will respond to you, refer you to other clubs or associations—maybe even pay you. If you are serious about making money on the platform, you will overcome whatever shyness would keep you from the fairly simple task of asking people for service club leads.

Give It All You've Got!

Another danger point during the early phases of starting an avocational speaking business is the subtle temptation to think of your free speeches as rehearsals for the really important speeches you will give later for large and financially generous audiences. Wrong! Those first speeches are, in many ways, the most important speeches you will ever give. They test your ability to speak with a sharp focus on the intersection of your knowledge and the audience's receptivity. They give you the opportunity to fine-tune your ideas and to experiment with the finely crafted definitions, explanations, metaphors, stories, transitions, and other stylistic devices that drive your speech upward from very good to outstanding. Your most promising strategy is to perfect one—only one—presentation to the point that it can't get any better. Then move on to another topic to which you can bring the rhetorical skills you developed in your first speech. Ten professional speakers out of ten will affirm that the quality of your materials and delivery constitutes your very best marketing tool.

While your family and friends may encourage you and help you fine-tune your presentation, you will be most fortunate to belong to a Toastmasters club, where a community of caring and insightful people will be glad to critique your presentation. Just about every club is willing to modify its schedule to accommodate a member who needs to rehearse a speech for an upcoming community presentation and will provide a pointed and helpful evaluation.

By giving the best speech you are capable of, videotaped repeatedly and infinitely fine-tuned as to both content and delivery, you can so impress your audiences that people will tell some other person about you, and that person will tell someone else—a ripple effect. When that happens, you will get invitations from people you never heard of to speak to groups you didn't know existed. You will discover what many speakers, even those in the high-fee bracket, have discovered—that free, high-quality speaking engagements are eminently worth doing. They provide opportunity to try out your material and possibly to reach some decision maker in your audience who will invite you to speak at a future time and place.

BASIC MARKETING STEPS FOR YOUR FIRST BOOKING

Make an Excellent Presentation

When you have a presentation that is geared to your audience, creatively prepared, and skillfully delivered, you have taken the first and most important step to getting on the platforms of your community—for pleasure or for profit. That is the first step of any speaker's marketing campaign.

Connect with the Decision Maker

The second step is to talk to the person who is the decision maker—ultimately the only way to get action on anything you may be selling. You can certainly communicate on the phone or, better yet, meet your prospect in person. Your primary task is to discern the felt needs of the group you want to address. By careful questioning, you can get past the answer you will hear often, "Oh, our folks are interested in just about any topic." Check to see how your topic or topics would fit that group. If repeated attempts to reach your prospect fails, you can send a letter of inquiry and follow up with a phone call. A sample letter of inquiry appears in Appendix I. A final approach could be sending a one-pager that provides the necessary information and following that up with a phone call.

Create a One-Pager

You will need that one-pager as you expand your marketing efforts. It should include (1) your name; (2) the topic or topics of your presentations with a brief description of each, written to highlight how that topic will impact the audience; and (3) your address, phone and fax numbers, and your e-mail and web address if you are online. After you have spoken a few times, you can add sentences of praise by people who have heard you, including their names and titles. To obtain these commendations, ask the meeting planner and audience members to complete an evaluation sheet at the close of your presentation. In addition, ask the meeting planner to write you an applause letter, putting in writing the compliments you received after you spoke. Generally, the meeting planner is more than willing to write you a letter at your request, expressing appreciation for the excellent job you did. Your picture is optional on a one-pager but useful if it is professionally done.

To design your one-pager, use the appropriate template on your word processor or, if you have graphic design talent, create your own. You may find companies like Paper Direct [(800) 272-7377] that provide predesigned brochure shells printed in color and ready for your promotional copy. They even offer software matched to their formats. However, engaging a first-class graphic artist to do the layout and choose the type is certainly worth its cost. The design should be simple and tasteful, printed on white or off-white paper with black ink so that it is easily faxable. Don't hesitate to ask for help at a Kinko's, Sir Speedy, or local print shop. An excellent example of a speaker's one-pager appears in Appendix N.

Be Introduced Well

The program planner will usually ask you for some biographical material. Write it as a script of introduction for the group's leader. Few service club officers possess the skill it takes to introduce a guest speaker properly, much less have the time to prepare for it. Many do not even realize that they have a responsibility to their own members to prepare them for the speaker's message. A few are good at the task, but most do it poorly. The speaker, therefore, must take the responsibility to be sure that the audience has the information it needs to respond optimally to the presentation—and in a form that works.

Be sure to take a copy with you for those all-too-frequent occasions when the speaker introduction you mailed a week in advance somehow never makes it to the meeting. Sometimes the introducer will put your material aside and ad lib your introduction—inadequately. You will learn to cope. A sample speaker introduction appears in Appendix M.

While the simple act of introducing you may not seem important, it helps establish your credibility, both for the speech and for your long-range objective of establishing a reputation as an expert presenter.

These four elements—(1) an excellent speech, (2) a personal contact or phone call, (3) a one-pager, and (4) a skillful introduction—are all you really need to get a good start. Once you have developed some momentum, you can begin to use some advanced forms of marketing.

SECOND-LEVEL MARKETING STEPS

Embedded Promotion

You can enhance your initial, direct marketing efforts with some subtle marketing that is—or seems to be—an integral part of your presentation. For example, you can include an oblique reference to a group you spoke to on a different topic, suggesting both your versatility and your availability. Your well-chosen first-person stories do a great deal to raise your credibility, making you an attractive choice as a speaker elsewhere. If you do consulting, your success stories provide a powerful suggestion to engage you as a consultant.

Publicity

A very few service clubs have members responsible for news releases to local newspapers; their members attend or stay away for reasons having nothing to do with newspaper publicity. However, you would be wise to submit a news release about your speaking engagement, with the meeting planners' permission. If you are unskilled at writing a standard news release or unsure as to whom to send it and when, check out a basic journalism book at your local library. Examine the format of the newspaper you are targeting. If it prints one or two sentences about club programs, provide one or two sentences. Send a longer piece to the paper that is likely to use it and add your photo if it is of professional quality. Generally, large newspapers are more likely to print shorter articles; smaller, local papers will give you more space. Inquire if the editor prefers your release to arrive by mail, fax, or e-mail.

Getting your article and picture in the paper as often as possible is well worth the cost of a professional photo and a well-written news release. It will begin to develop your image in the community as a speaker, and it has a high likelihood of evoking requests for other speaking engagements. If the club publishes a newsletter, submit your release to its editor, asking that a file copy be sent to you. You will find a place to use it in subsequent marketing efforts.

If you are speaking on a topic of broad appeal, or even on something very specialized but interesting to the general public, ask your local newspaper to interview you. Ask your radio station to have you as a guest on a talk show. Editors are constantly looking for new people, services, ideas, and products; that is how they make their living. You can help both them and yourself by making yourself known.

The impact of an occasional article you publish will certainly bring your name to the attention of people who book speakers. Look at your local newspaper to see what area of business is neglected, and offer to write a regular column—an even stronger marketing ploy. You may reach additional people by obtaining reprints of your article or column. Use them for a direct mail campaign or as inserts in your correspondence.

Ask if the service club that engages you has a good photographer with high-quality equipment who can take your picture, preferably with its president or a member who is well known in the community. If no photographer is available and you can afford to hire one, do it. Order several additional prints. You may send them with your news releases to promote subsequent speaking engagements.

Evaluation Forms

Some of the material you use for your one-pager will come from members of the audience who complete an evaluation form, assuming that they sign it and give you permission to quote them. More important, their evaluations will give you valuable information that will shorten your learning curve. Prepare a simple, short form to be placed at each seat and, before you begin, alert them to it. Tell them that you are committed to continuous improvement of your speaking and that you would appreciate a few minutes of their time to help you after you have finished your presentation. You can ask them to rate you from 1 to 10 or on a continuum of excellent/good/fair. Use only a few criteria such as clarity of your ideas, use of stories, and your delivery skill. The main benefit, however, will come from open-ended questions like "To what extent did the presentation meet your expectations?" or "What did you like most/least about the speech?" While you will profit from every evaluation, it is these responses that will help you grow as a speaker and a marketer. A sample evaluation form is found in Appendix L.

Networking

Arrive early enough to network during the minutes before the meeting starts, walking around to meet people and engaging in conversation with the persons you sit next to. Stay as long as people remain after the meeting. Ask questions about their work and community involvements, listening for a hook into another speaking engagement. Offer your business card and request theirs, annotating the back for items of information about them that you can use in a follow-up call. Use this information to develop a database to extend your speaking opportunities, anticipating a direct mail effort at some time in the future. You may also use the information to sell products or services connected with your primary business—if they are relevant to your speech—or to offer books and tapes you will develop from your topics. If you do not start collecting business cards and developing a database early in your career, you will lament the lost contacts when you need them most.

Networking will produce leads and also information about the pains, challenges, and frustrations of the people you meet. Enriching your material or developing new topics requires a keen understanding of peoples' struggles. Keep a notebook of what you hear so that when you are ready to change or enlarge your topic list you will be dealing with business or personal situations that are genuine and, incidentally, salable.

In addition to getting names for future marketing and ideas for speech material, networking should also produce referrals. You will get a referral by asking audience members for one during your postpresentation networking: "Do you know of a group that might profit from hearing me speak on this topic?" Get the name of both the group and a contact person with a phone number—and permission to use the name of the person who gave it to you. Then follow up on this information by offering yourself as a speaker.

Say Thank You

Conclude your relationship with the club by sending a brief thank-you note to the person who engaged you or to the club president. You will join a tiny minority of speakers who are savvy enough to know the rewards of that modest activity. You are just about guaranteed that your note will be read aloud at the next meeting, reinforcing the members' memory of the wonderful presentation you made. It might even remind some company president in the audience to invite you to speak to an employee group (for a fee!). The few minutes it takes to write a note of thanks and the price of a postage stamp could pay off handsomely.

FROM FREE TO FEE AND BACK AGAIN

At what point does the beginning speaker begin to earn money on the platform? At some point, if you are staying busy with speaking dates, you will feel the need to get paid for your efforts. That magic moment when you charge your first fee may occur when you respond to a request by saying, "My schedule is getting so full that I have begun charging a fee for speaking." On the other hand, a request for information about your fee may come from an audience member or someone who has heard about you, perhaps on the assumption that you regularly charge a fee. Name it: $50 or $250 or $500 or what seems appropriate for the situation. You may have to use a little trial and error so that you are not underestimating or overestimating your value. What you have to say might be worth $100 at a Chamber of Commerce luncheon in New Albany, Mississippi, or $1,000 at the Chamber in Phoenix, Arizona. At first, you may simply have to ask what the group's usual fee is. If you lose a booking because your fee is so low that they think you are unqualified or because you are ridiculously above their means, learn from your experience and do better next time.

> I decided I wanted to get into speaking because I wanted to do seminars; I thought it was one of my talents. I realized I needed to do more speaking so I talked to every Rotary, Optimist, and Exchange Club I could. Finally I was asked to do a talk for a hair salon to tell their stylists how to promote themselves and how to stay motivated. And I got $200 for doing that gig. I must have given hundreds of service club talks. I didn't give my first paid talk until after my first NSA convention in 1982, and I've been at it ever since.
>
> **Michael A. Podolinsky** is principal of Team Seminars of Eden Prairie, Minnesota.

When you get to the higher fee bracket, you may have to engage in some negotiating. You can simply lower your fee to what the client's budget allows, offer to add an informal breakout session if they meet your fee, or even speak twice on the program. You might barter your time for some goods or services you need, coming away with no dollars but some software or a set of new tires. You might throw in a workbook for each participant to sweeten the deal or make such arrangements as your business sense leads you to. From there on, the setting of your fee becomes a matter of supply and demand. The more requests you get, the higher your fee can go. Stay on the conservative side, however. In the long run, you will be busier if you are at or just below the going rate for speakers on your topic and at your level of speaking experience.

Don't think for a minute that once you have started to charge for your speaking engagements you can never return to free appearances. The normal progression of moving from free to fee involves a period when you will do both. Even persons who gave up their day job to make a highly profitable living on the platform are offered opportunities to speak to groups without compensation, and they will jump at the chance if they know that people in that audience are in a position to hire them for a significant fee. As an avocational speaker, you will have to sort out which of those "freebies" you can afford to turn down—hardly any—and which ones you will be delighted to accept. In general, follow the principle that you will speak any time, any place, at any price, including none. You will obtain bookings to the extent that you are a recognized commodity—an outstanding speaker who can be counted on to deliver the goods consistently. Remember that every group you speak to adds X number of people who can pass on your name to people who can hire you.

TREAT YOUR SPEAKING AS A BUSINESS

If you are serious about avocational speaking, you will treat your speaking as a business and not as a hobby. Like every other successful business, you need a mission statement and a set of goals that will carry out your mission. Your mission statement should begin by stating the *why* of your speaking activity. Don't hesitate to articulate your reason in terms of deeply felt concerns about your topic and your audiences. It is your passion that will propel you most surely toward your goal. The goal should state what it is you plan to achieve in a given time period—at least as to the number of speaking dates and income. As you grow, you may wish to enlarge the scope of the goals to include the *how*—the strategies by which you plan to reach the goals. Keep the mission statement simple and the goals realistic, but don't omit this step.

Make a Name for Yourself

In many states, you can adopt a business name with minimum red tape; in others you may have to pay a fee to register with the state government. Many speakers call themselves something like Jane Smith and Associates or The Antonelli Group, even if the associates or group consists of their family, support group, or other speakers to whom they can refer business when they are too busy to handle it all.

Take Your Graphic Image Seriously

It is no longer too expensive to employ first-class graphics for your business cards and letterhead. The technology in your own office probably provides a wide range of type fonts and templates you can use with minimum skill. However, many neighborhood print shops now equal large commercial printing companies in their ability to design and print tasteful, high-quality work. Whether it seems fair to you or not, decision makers connect the quality of your printing to the quality of your speaking. Within reason, the money you spend on high-quality business printing is well worth the cost.

Keep Accurate Records

You will find it useful to set up a simple system for keeping track of your speaking business. It may involve a few file folders or some fairly complex software to fill your marketing and accounting needs. Here's why you need accurate records.

One reason to keep accurate records is that you need to keep your prospect list alive. It is easy to lose track of the potential buyers who are the lifeblood of your business. Writing names and phone numbers on little bits of paper or on a tablet almost condemns that information to oblivion. Many inexpensive databases are now available for your computer. Enter into a phone/address list everyone who has the potential to help you—prospective meeting planners, people who have heard you speak (especially those who can recommend you), support group members like Toastmasters, a church or synagogue fellowship group, or members of an NSA chapter. Don't write off people who have said no to you; you will get back to them. You will have sent them a thank-you note for having spoken with you, letting them know that you hope to be of help to them at a later time. When you revise your one-pager with a new topic or a new applause letter, send them a copy. It is axiomatic in selling that prospects need to see your name several times before they even begin to consider a purchase.

Another reason to keep accurate records is that you need to know what's working for you—which activities bring in business and which do not. Impressions and memories fade; records remain. Keep a record of business cards you hand out; how many, where, and to whom. Then follow up on the promising leads. Note the responses you get to any direct mail efforts. Keep track of the frequency, type, and location of your speaking dates to discover what patterns of success are developing or what gaps you may need to fill.

Yet another reason to be in the record-keeping mode is that you may have some recognition coming. If you are a Toastmaster working for a Competent Toastmaster (CTM) or an Advanced Toastmaster (ATM) designation, you must keep accurate records to be signed by the club's vice president of education. If you choose to benefit from membership in the National Speakers Association, which requires 10 paid speaking engagements on your application, you are obliged to verify those engagements with records. The NSA doesn't ask how much you made or when; they do ask for documentation. Even if your present goals as a speaker are modest, you may well develop a significant enterprise later on. Earning the NSA's designation as a Certified Speaking Professional (CSP), requires a great deal of paperwork, but the status you receive will make keeping accurate records worthwhile. That designation is available equally to full-time and to avocational speakers.

Keeping records is also essential for accuracy in completing tax returns. Your income, even as an avocational speaker, may become substantial. You will have speaking-related expenses, including mileage and a home office, and you will need records in case the IRS requires an audit. The IRS makes booklets and people available to answer your questions about deductions, and you can engage an accountant for more complex tax matters. Start by purchasing a bookkeeping book or an inexpensive software program such as Quicken, available from most office supplies stores.

A good start to a record-keeping system would include the following:

- Your prospect list with notes on what happens with each contact you make.
- Marketing materials you use and develop, starting with a one-pager.
- A media list of newspapers, magazines, and radio and television stations that can help you keep your name in the public eye.
- Correspondence, including letters confirming the arrangements, letters of thanks, and letters of commendation you receive (a sample confirmation letter appears in Appendix J).
- Contracts with meeting planners when you are speaking for a fee (a sample contract appears in Appendix K).
- Financial records or summaries of their content.
- A marketing idea bank.
- An ever-expanding idea file for new topics and supporting material.

KEEP YOUR LIFE IN BALANCE

Building a part-time speaking career is an exciting and rewarding experience, but it can consume you if you don't keep it in balance with the rest of your life. Surviving in our world is stressful enough, given the necessity of excelling in your primary job, educating and nurturing children, saving for retirement, contributing to community life, and nurturing your spirit. You don't need to go crazy becoming a speaker.

Develop a clear mission for your whole life—yourself and the people who mean the most to you. Include the activities, money, energy, and time commitment it will take to help speaking contribute to your goals. Then do what it takes to make it. Just make sure that your mission includes taking care of yourself—mind, body, and spirit—and that you take care of the people who make the rest of your life worthwhile.

Intelligent, energetic, and creative people often have difficulty selecting one activity, one career, one goal. If you're like me, you've probably enjoyed several different professions, often simultaneously. Currently, I'm employed full time as an associate professor in the School of Human Services in Springfield College, Massachusetts, operate a part-time (20-hours-a-week) speaking and consulting business, and serve as contract manager for a small Employee Assistance Program. While on the surface these projects may appear to be unrelated, each fits into my overall mission—to bring respect to workers, facilitate women's contributions to corporate America, and create healthy workplaces.

How do I combine these diverse activities? Perhaps even more important, how do I balance my life? My answer is loving what I do and doing what I love. I have a zeal for keeping in perspective both people and profits. You might wonder how I find the time to do everything. Fortunately, because I teach two weekends a month and have a flexible weekday schedule, I am free to pursue whatever activities are most pressing—whether grading papers, writing articles, or making a presentation.

Make no mistake, I also put a priority on self-care. I exercise daily, either swimming outdoors when the weather permits or walking. I limit my food intake of sugar and fats and get six or more hours of sleep. Moreover, I take time to read spiritual literature, meditate, write in a journal, and attend 12-step recovery meetings.

Whether to remain a part-time professional speaker continues to tickle my brain, especially as the speaking engagements and consulting contracts flourish. Becoming a nationally known keynoter is seductive. So I remind myself of my personal values. At the top of my list are being with family and friends, swimming in the pond, playing with the dog, and sleeping in my own bed at night. I'm happy; I enjoy my lifestyle; I make an adequate income that provides for all my needs; and I help people to meet their goals and find satisfaction at work. I still have trouble selecting one thing to do, but I have a strong focus and am committed to this mission.

Nancy C. Zare is on the faculty of Springfield College in Springfield, Massachusetts, and is principal in N-Vision Z, a consulting firm.

8 Full-Time Speakers

A front-page column in the *Wall Street Journal* several years ago highlighted the huge fees being paid to celebrity speakers, contrasting them with what the writer called "no-name speakers." The reporter wrote

> For every Norman Schwartzkopf or Margaret Thatcher raking in highly publicized speaking fees of up to $80,000 per banquet, hundreds of low-budget lecturers claw to be heard on everything from algebra-made-easy to Zen dentistry. On any given night, up to 7,000 speakers step up to podiums in the U.S.—60% of them for pay—according to estimates by booking agents. Some 70,000 would-be keynoters are chasing those jobs, and 300 hopefuls sign up with local speakers bureaus every week.[1]

The journalistic style of Robert Johnson may contain a dollop of cynicism to produce engaging copy, but he certainly caught the public's interest in professional speaking. Who are these "no-name speakers" and what have they to do with you? They are today's professional speakers, each of whom really does have a name—although perhaps not that of a celebrity. They are important people in today's economy.

WHAT IS FULL-TIME, PROFESSIONAL SPEAKING?

Speakers, avocational and full-time, are growing in number every year. As the meetings industry expands with ever-larger numbers of people attending growing numbers of business gatherings, more speakers are taking their places before audiences. In recent years, paid platform speakers have adopted the term *professional speaker.*

In one sense, speaking is professional when the speaker brings to the marketplace a service for which money is paid. In another, speaking is professional when it is consistently, predictably excellent. By that measure, avocational and celebrity speaking may be professional speaking. But people who are making their entire living by speaking on the platform consider themselves professional in the sense that they have become a distinct category of employed people. Ask them what they do for a living and they will answer, "I am a professional speaker." And so they are.

However, if you restrict "full-time, professional speakers" to the definition they had a decade or two ago—persons whose work is confined to giving motivational, "keynote" addresses to large business gatherings—their numbers are shrinking. The reality of today's speaking business is that platform speakers in the business and association market are increasingly deriving their income not only from speaking but also from training, consulting, and the sale of products such as tapes and books. Nearly a dozen of them are adding to their mixes by offering seminars and learning products on how to become professional speakers. For the sake of convenience, the terms *professional speaker* and *full-time speaker* will be used interchangeably.

The founders of the National Speakers Association in the mid-1970s were, for the most part, avocational speakers, giving keynote addresses to business and association audiences or addressing them as lecturers on specialized topics. They were speaker-entrepreneurs whose popularity enabled them to be successful on a full-time basis. Cavett Robert, the NSA's founding father, was a successful attorney who kept taking on more speaking assignments until he concluded that a career on the platform would be more rewarding. Carl Winters, a Baptist pastor in the Chicago suburb of Oak Park, became such a successful part-time speaker that General Motors hired him as a full-time motivational speaker for employee groups and for community groups, where he created a positive image for GM. He became the second president of the National Speakers Association.

Between then and now, most of those early speakers and the people who followed have broadened their communication activities to what some people are calling, perhaps a bit inelegantly, information merchandising. The platform styles of the most highly visible speakers range from highly entertaining, stimulating, motivational presentations to profound lectures on serious subjects. Many of them also consult with clients, most widely in the area of business communication, sales skills, and management principles and strategies. They may sell audio or video recordings of their presentations to audience members or to people in their databases, using direct mail or the Internet. A growing number of them publish newsletters, write columns for popular or trade publications, and provide fax-on-demand services. Many provide specialized information through a link on their web sites. Still others appear on business shows in the cable or satellite television format. Wisely, they have developed these ways to even out their income. There may still be a small number of speakers who make their living by giving 30- to 90-minute motivational or humorous presentations—doing no training or consulting and having no products for sale—but they are relatively few.

Most of today's full-time, professional speakers began their careers as avocational speakers—many of them developing their skills in Toastmasters clubs—and worked up to full-time status. They went through something like the process described in the preceding chapter until they were able to support themselves totally. For many of them, the process took two to five years. Their numbers increased dramatically in the 1980s and 1990s, significantly raising the competitive stakes and forcing them to discover creative ways to market themselves and their corollary services and products. Those who are succeeding are nimble enough to satisfy the requirements of a changing, demanding marketplace.

Contributing to the variety and size of the professional speaker pool are the large number of women taking their place in the workforce and the ever-increasing fluidity of that workforce. While nearly all the professional speakers in the 1970s were men, approximately half the speakers on today's platforms are women. Many people who have left their jobs because of downsizing and mergers—or are simply undergoing a career change—have successfully moved to the platform as a rewarding venue for sharing their energy, information, and skills with various publics.

It is important to be clear about the word *professional* as it applies to speakers. While it suggests receiving money for speaking, it also correctly denotes an attitude that values high standards of preparation and delivery. An avocational speaker who practices law or teaches college for a living may be just as professional a speaker as someone whose entire income derives from the platform and its corollary businesses. So also is a speaker who speaks without any fee at all, providing valuable information to the public as a community service or on behalf of an employer or sponsor. Indeed, without professional standards of marketing and performing, no one can stay in front of audiences for very long.

WHO ARE THE FULL-TIME PROFESSIONAL SPEAKERS?

The following categories may be useful in understanding the variety of platform speakers, but they should not be viewed as air-tight categories. Each is a rough approximation that suggests a cluster of similar competencies, topics, and techniques shared by speakers. However, most professional speakers blend several qualities into their presentations.

Advocates

Advocates hold a strong opinion on a subject and utilize persuasive speaking techniques to obtain a decision. Their goal is to move their audiences from saying no to an idea or a course of action to agreement with that idea or to the action they are advocating. Salespeople are advocates, whether selling $7.95 vegetable peelers at the county fair or million-dollar computer systems to a Fortune 500 company or government agency. Evangelists are advocates, calling their listeners to a religious conversion. Politicians are advocates, seeking votes to take them to the city council, state house of representatives, or the White House.

On the business platform, all kinds of companies and associations employ speakers who can articulate the reasons for supporting a cause in which they believe strongly or for buying a product or service. Their arena is sales and marketing. A sales or marketing representative for the Boeing corporation may appear before audiences in a region that is likely to profit from the company's receiving a government contract for a new line of airplanes. The purpose is to encourage listeners to put pressure on Washington decision makers. A metropolitan tourist and convention center may send a speaker to a convention of travel agents to drum up interest in getting more tourists to visit that speaker's city. A speaker representing a chain of lifecare communities may speak to a group of senior adults about their options for living in the retirement years, one of which is to live in a community operated by that corporation.

While advocates may be full-time professional speakers, advocacy speaking is also done by celebrity and avocational speakers. Sarah Brady is a powerful advocate for gun control, an excellent speaker whose husband, James Brady, President Reagan's press secretary, was permanently disabled in the assassination attempt on the president's life. Her platform presentations did a great deal to achieve the passage of the so-called Brady Bill, which strictly limits handgun sales. Many celebrities, like Robert Kennedy, Jr., are advocates for the environment. His cousin, Edward Kennedy, Jr., who lost a leg to cancer as a child, advocates programs for the disabled, frequently raising a great deal of money for that cause. Among the most popular causes to bring Hollywood personalities to the platform is AIDS, one of whose earliest advocates was the actress Elizabeth Taylor. Advocates of this kind may donate their time and expenses; some speak for reimbursement of expenses only; others receive a generous fee plus expenses. The money may come from the inviting group or from a benefactor who shares the group's passion for the cause.

Speaker-Celebrities

Some motivational speakers have developed such a high degree of competence and marketing skill that their names have become household words—Zig Ziglar and Tony Robbins, for example. Their ability to entertain audiences while enlightening them has made them crowd pleasers in great demand. Their frequent appearances over vast geographical areas and over a long period of time, combined with their book and tape sales, have made their names identifiable whenever people talk about professional speakers. Professional motivational speakers who attempt to explain to their relatives what they do for a living frequently hear, "Oh, just like Zig Ziglar!"

There is another sense in which all paid speakers are celebrity speakers of a sort. The very presence of a guest speaker on a convention program grants that speaker a measure of celebrity status. Contributing to that measure is the flyer including the speaker's photograph that goes to association members, student mail boxes, and corporate e-mail addresses. The introduction of the speaker by the master of ceremonies is designed to set the speaker above the audience in terms of subject matter expertise or status in the business community. If the speaker sells a book or a set of tapes at the back of the room, audience members line up to have the product autographed, as they would if the speaker were a celebrated sports figure or the country's First Lady.

Humorists

Enjoying a period of hearty laughter, especially at the closing banquet of a heavy convention, is a common goal of meeting planners for business associates and corporations. For college audiences, a program of hilarious fun is a predictably big draw. Some celebrities can provide these programs of comedy, but professional speakers who fit this market niche are plentiful.

Humorists generally differentiate themselves from comedians. Comedians perform purely for the sake of evoking laughter, certainly a worthwhile aim. On the other hand, humorists use funny material to make a point—perhaps the way humor makes the workplace a more effective and productive environment, or humor as a means to relieve stress. Many humorists teach a business lesson on customer service or self-esteem with a presentation that is 90 percent to 95 percent humorous material. Humorist Steve Rizzo of New

York gives a talk on "The Seven Attitudes of Humor," applying each one to a means of stress reduction in the workplace. Popular speakers who do not bill themselves as humorists may use a great deal of it and are sometimes booked largely because of the entertaining dimension of their programs.

Liz Curtis Higgs gives a humorous presentation, "One Laugh to Live!—A Light-Hearted Look at the Stress-Relieving, Health-Enhancing Power of Humor." Like other successful humorists, she uses topical humor adapted to the client's situations, humor based on this morning's news, and the humor of tried and true stories guaranteed to evoke laughter. Dave Petitjean says his "gift is tickling your funny bone with a fresh, honest-to-goodness family-type Cajun humor." Jeanne Robertson, a former Miss North Carolina, is a legendary humorist who bills herself as "A Tall Speaker with a Tall Sense of Humor." Robert Henry specializes in blending clean humor with inspirational messages for banquets and seminars. For people willing to grow, Grady Jim Robinson offers deep psychological insights through his uncanny ability to move them with his humorous stories. Dale Irvin has become a fixture at NSA conventions, offering humorous commentary on the day's events—a skill he takes to corporate and association meetings.

Motivational Speakers

Unlike advocates who work to significantly *change* peoples' opinions—corporate marketers, evangelists, or sales presenters—motivational speakers seek to *reinforce* values that their audience members already hold. They know that their audiences believe in hard work, loyalty, integrity, self-worth, patriotism, tolerance, optimism, and other virtues. Like the people who hire them as speakers, they also know that those values need to be strengthened to the point that people function more effectively and obtain a greater sense of satisfaction from their activities and their relationships.

Generally, meeting planners engage a motivational speaker because the meeting they are planning is designed to increase productivity for a company or a deeper sense of commitment to the goals and programs of an association or a profession. The most successful motivational speakers articulate the appropriate virtues with colorful, sensory, metaphorical language and illustrate their talks with a combination of personal experiences and stories from the world of work, seeking to move the audience to a higher degree of commitment. A personal experience story that opens the speech is called a *signature story.* The talk itself is generally called a keynote speech because it is designed to strike just the right note for the meetings and breakout sessions that follow. Sometimes, a motivational speaker will be asked to close the convention, again sounding the right note that will send attendees off, fired up and ready for the challenges that will face them.

A few minutes of browsing through the NSA Directory or a sheaf of flyers in a speakers bureau's file cabinet will reveal some of the topics of motivational speakers. Each of these speakers uses a unique approach to the topic, generally developed out of considerable experience in the business world. Each speaker is unique in the choice of success and failure stories. The stories are highly personal; the best titles brief and enticing.

- "Make Every Day a Terrific Day," Ed Foreman of Dallas, Texas
- "See You at the Top," Zig Ziglar of Carrollton, Texas
- "Attitudes Are Contagious—Are Yours Worth Catching?" Dennis E. Mannering of Green Bay, Wisconsin
- "How to Reprogram Your Mind for Success in 30 Days," Pam Lontos of Laguna Hills, California
- "Straight Talk Is More Than Words," Patricia Ball of St. Louis, Missouri
- "Self-Esteem: The Bottom Line in Employee Motivation and Productivity," Hanoch McCarty of Galt, California

- "Be All That You Can Be!" Debra Crumpton of Sacramento, California
- "A Strategy for Winning," Carl Mays of Gatlinburg, Tennessee
- "How to Stay on the Cutting Edge without Losing Your Balance," Glenna Salsbury of Paradise Valley, Arizona

How does a speaker develop a motivational presentation? The process generally develops from the speaker's own experience of having accomplished some level of achievement or having overcome a disability, physical or otherwise. It may begin with a motto or a slogan; a single, strong metaphor; or a current event that is on everyone's mind and that might require some unpacking. If the marketplace seems hospitable to the message, the speaker develops a main idea and subsidiary ideas, all supported by stories, provocative ideas, quotations, or material that comprises a strong presentation.

Personal Development Speakers

While motivational speakers work to move people toward greater achievement, personal development speakers focus on the individual's inner life. They are sometimes called *inspirational speakers*. Self-esteem is one of the more popular topics that attract meeting planners. People whose egos have been bruised by overly critical parents or teachers or negative life experiences need to be assured that they have inner resources they have not begun to tap.

Managing personal stress and achieving a balance between business and family life are other topics addressed by personal development speakers. Speakers in the 1990s found fertile ground for presentations on spirituality—not on religion—but on a rapidly developing awareness that there is more to life than big salaries, powerful cars, exotic vacations, and large homes. Not only have these assets become inflated in importance, these speakers assert, but they have obscured the divine source of those gifts. Speakers on spirituality call attention to the successes of the 12-step movements that call on a higher power for strength. They note the books, movies, and television shows on angels; the social movements driven by spiritually motivated groups; and the rapid growth of religious groups that call forth the development of the inner self. Canadian Ian Percy and Frank Bucaro of Illinois center many of their addresses to business audiences around themes of spirituality, connecting with their insights on business ethics or a positive corporate culture.

Some speakers develop their careers in part or entirely on speaking to religious groups, generally including—but not limited to—their own faith tradition. Some are clergypersons or former clergypersons whose appeal is broad enough for them to address a variety of denominational groups. The late clergyman and author Norman Vincent Peale was welcome in a wide variety of religious groups but was almost more popular at business gatherings. Likewise, Robert Schuller, pastor of the Crystal Cathedral in Garden Grove, California, is an immensely popular speaker. Another clergyman and college professor in great demand as a speaker to business groups is Tony Campolo of Eastern College in Pennsylvania.

Lay persons also develop topics around the increasingly popular topic of spirituality. Deepak Chopra, M.D., specializes in linking spirituality with health. Canadian speaker Robin S. Sharma writes,

> Say goodbye to re-engineering and re-invention. The hottest business trends of the future are people-centered: loyalty, teams, spirituality. . . . Spirituality is not about bringing religion into the workplace; it is personal discovery, building synergy and seeing work and life as an adventure that liberates the brilliance that lies within us all.[2]

Among the best-known NSA speakers in this category are Florence Littauer and Joanne Wallace, who offer inspirational addresses that are popular in both the religious and the business communities.

The difference between personal development and motivational speeches is, of course, not at all rigid and sometimes not at all clear. Speakers who can do one can do the other equally well. Indeed, any given presentation may combine the two. To complicate the distinction further, a demand is rising for speakers on ethics in business and government, suggesting a purely informational presentation on what the law or corporate policy requires. Lawyers are filling many of these speaking dates, but speakers who deal in human values may well root their advice on ethical questions in spirituality. Listeners to any of these speakers will make up their own minds as to how they receive the message: a personal development speech may heighten the listener's sense of worth, increasing one's sales performance; a motivational message may drive another listener inward to explore untapped spiritual resources. Even a straight lecture on the law may be given with spiritual sensitivity.

First-Person Performers/Speakers

Ralph Archbold of Philadelphia has spent about a quarter of a century as Benjamin Franklin, fully costumed and extremely well informed about the life of one of American history's most colorful figures. Unlike some of his imitators, who walk around Independence Hall smiling, shaking hands, and being photographed, Archbold is foremost a speaker on many of the same topics as other business speakers—leadership, managing change, working with difficult people—but always in Franklin's own words or in words that reflect Franklin's approach to life. Joan Janssen Nietsche takes on the persona of Empress Catherine the Great, speaking on "How to Be a

Super Star with Women Customers" and "Beating the Burnout Blues." George Velliotes, a humorist with a message, takes on many personalities, depending on audience requirements: Sir Thomas Bagley-White, British Health Minister; Lonny Rogers, Southern prison warden; Sheik Salaam, Saudi Arabian oil chief; or some other outrageous character. These first-person speakers straddle the line between acting and speaking, but most are primarily speakers who use the character they have adopted as a marketing tool or a device to handle their topic in a creative way.

Business Experts

Clearly the largest number of professional speakers fit the category of experts in some phase of business. The categories that follow are relatively discreet, but many of them blend into others in any given presentation.

- Change
- Leadership
- Customer service
- Etiquette, protocol
- Management, supervision
- Creative problem solving
- Image, fashion
- Ethics and values
- Diversity
- Personal development
- Sales and marketing
- Communication skills: speaking and writing
- Strategic planning
- The future
- Global market, intercultural dimensions
- Time management
- Addictions

- Gender communication
- Team building
- Stress management
- Marketing
- Success/achievement
- Health
- Empowerment
- Productivity
- Quality
- Technology
- Interpersonal relationships

Education Speakers

Most of us remember going to high school assembly programs where we were offered good advice by a visiting speaker. Education speakers are still doing a vigorous business, helping today's students hear what they would not hear from their own teachers or parents.

Dick Gallagher of Philadelphia, a former public school teacher, has developed a profitable speaking career with his presentations to students on "How to Study." He also addresses evening parent gatherings and does dozens of in-service days for teachers throughout the school year. Michael Scott Karpovich of Michigan markets himself as one who speaks to, for, and about children. He asserts that "Nerds Rule" and "Yuk Makes You Stronger." Always wearing his trademark—different colored tennis shoes—he bills himself as half Robin Williams and half Leo Buscaglia.

John Alston of Los Angeles speaks on "Surviving the School Game." He says,

> You have not been truly challenged until you have stepped into a gymnasium or auditorium of twenty-five

hundred or more teenagers and held their attention for an hour. I use this one speech to cover issues ranging from parent–teacher relationships, personal responsibility, character, and more. Each issue requires its own attending story or example.[3]

In addition to free-lance speakers like Alston are speakers sponsored by organizations that want to influence student opinion or action in a specific way, for instance, concerning drug use or safe sex.

College and University Speakers

College and university students constitute a huge market. Almost all of the more than thirty-five hundred institutions of higher learning bring outside entertainment and lecture programs to their campuses each year. About twelve hundred of these colleges are members of the National Association for Campus Activities (NACA), founded to facilitate the booking of entertainers. This association's national and regional conventions bring together performers and campus representatives who book those performers—both students and staff members of student activities offices. Performers showcase their talents at these meetings and make themselves available in trade show booths.

The lecturers compete for dollars with the 85 percent to 90 percent of college performers who are entertainers—mostly rock and jazz musicians. Hypnosis and ESP practitioners join comedians, magicians, impressionists, jugglers, dancers, stiltwalkers, balloon sculptors, rope jumpers, sound and light programs, and zany basketball teams to attract student audiences. Interactive games are one of the newest attractions for student groups. A handful of presenters combine music and speech. An example is Robin Greenstein of

New York, who presents "Images of Women," which combines her talent of singing and playing folk music with her lectures on women's issues.

Celebrities are as popular on the college circuit as in the business community. But many lecturers have become profitable there, speaking on such topics as diversity, lifestyle issues, the environment, leadership, gender issues, addictions, career planning, and being successful in college and the world of work. An example of a lecturer on an ever-popular subject is 28-year-old Bradley Richardson, who speaks on "Jobsmarts for Twentysomethings: The Next Best Thing to Having a Trust Fund." Increasingly, professors are sensitive to the value of students hearing messages on topics that they are unqualified to speak about. Attendance as a course requirement is assigned at lectures given by visiting speakers. Hearing about the Vietnam War from a superb speaker who fought in it, for example, makes an impression no classroom lecture, textbook, or even a movie can match.

Success as a college speaker is not easy. The environment is drastically different from business and association speaking. Barry Drake, NACA's Lecturer of the Year in 1995 and 1996 for his program on the history of rock and roll, advises hopefuls to learn how to talk straight-on to students without a hint of condescension, to dress as students dress, and to forget their credentials. With his wife, who operates the audio and a glittering program of visuals, he is on the road 235 days a year. Not only can the schedule be demanding but also the competition is stiff. At a recent NACA regional conference, 480 performers competed for 54 showcase time periods. Fees for noncelebrity lecturers on the college circuit range from $500 to $2,500 an appearance. With the help of print pieces, telemarketing, and audio- and videotapes, many performers market themselves, while others work with booking agencies.

Trainers

Training is a job category by itself but is closely related to the speaking business. Trainers belong to one of three broad categories: (1) in-house trainers who are employed by corporations, (2) trainers who work for training companies that make them available to clients on a project basis, and (3) independent, entrepreneurial trainers. The overlap between speaking skills and training skills is so large that speakers and trainers find crossing between the two relatively easy. A detailed analysis of the similarities and differences appears in Chapter 4. While most corporately employed trainers and those who operate training businesses on their own do not think of themselves as speakers, most people who identify themselves as speakers are also trainers. Each speaker works out the ratio between the two activities partly on the basis of their enjoyment in doing one or the other, but more likely on the basis of what pays the best.

Seminar Leaders

The word *seminar* has broadened its meaning in recent years from a small group of university graduate students doing original research to just about any kind of educational experience. Employees of a movie theater chain may, for example, be required to take a "seminar" on increasing popcorn sales. If not led by one of that company's corporate trainers, it might well be led by an instructor from a training company or a free-lance speaker who also does sales training seminars. Those speakers who do training assignments generally characterize their presentations as seminars.

In the speaking business, seminars are also understood as public seminars, generally those put on by one of the national seminar companies, such as Career Track, SkillPath, Fred Pryor, Dun & Bradstreet, or the American Management Association. These companies market their seminars to huge mailing lists, sometimes attracting hundreds of people to a hotel meeting room for a low-cost, one-day learning experience. The charge generally ranges from $85 to $175. Attendees may learn anything from computer skills to dealing with difficult people. While each seminar company contracts with seminar leaders on slightly different terms, the leader earns from $200 to $500 per day, plus a commission on sales of books and tapes. Many full-time, professional speakers make an excellent living by contracting with these companies. The major public seminar companies are listed in Appendix C.

In the 1990s, a number of smaller companies began doing business on a local or regional level, issuing catalogs of their topics to geographically defined mailing lists, advertising in local media, and getting their trainers into guest appearances on local talk shows. *Sharing Ideas* magazine called them "new wave seminar companies." Many of them belong to the trade group, Center for Advancement of Lifelong Learning. Like the older national companies, they provide nonacademic learning for busy adults in half-day or full-day formats. Subjects offered include assertiveness training, using the Internet, gourmet cooking, surviving a divorce, etiquette for today, great ideas in great books, finding your ancestors, astrology, investing, and many more. Unlike the more traditional, national companies, they tend to offer their programs in the evenings and on weekends.

One of the largest in this new group is the Learning Annex, operating in several large cities. Its comment on the future of the seminar business is:

> The seminar business is the place to be right now! People are looking for a different way to conduct their lives,

> whether it be having less stress, learning about spirituality, meeting new people, or starting a small business. Seminar leaders who present this kind of information plus ancillary products can really find a niche in this industry.[4]

Both avocational and full-time speakers staff these programs.

Sponsored Speakers

Not all paid speakers derive their fees from the company, association, or college that provides them an audience. They are the *sponsored speakers,* sometimes called public relations speakers. Many nonprofit organizations engage celebrities or release their own executives to do fund-raising talks for research on AIDS, cancer, and heart, lung, and other diseases. Some people on the payroll of organizations concerned about world hunger, the environment, or other challenges to the world's well-being are hired to give advocacy talks. Many utilities arrange for their employees to speak to local civic groups, such as the Kiwanis Club, and senior audiences. They want the public to know what factors influence their water or electric bills, and they want to create a receptive attitude toward themselves in anticipation of the competition that increasing deregulation is bringing about. So important is the support of communities for their utilities that the Edison Electric Institute, a national trade group, convenes the utilities' community affairs managers in a speakers committee to facilitate these presentations.

Corporations also find it profitable to sponsor speakers. A notable example is the pharmaceutical industry, whose companies routinely sponsor presentations to medical and other health-care organizations by sending out physicians who are members of their research staffs or doctors in private practice who are using a manufacturer's products. Some, like SmithKline Beecham Pharmaceuticals, engage pharmacists or other qualified scientists to represent them. Jeff Mackie, a registered pharmacist with a Ph.D. in pharmacy and toxicology and director of product training at SmithKline, is a gifted speaker who presents highly entertaining motivational talks to the company's wholesale buyers in cooperation with its sales department. An active member of the National Speakers Association, he speaks on humor in the workplace, self-image, and self-esteem, gaining goodwill for his company.

Two other speaker groups enhance SmithKline's marketing. One is a team of 30 regional medical associates, all having Ph.D.s or Pharm.D.s, who provide full-time technical backup to the sales staff. They give presentations to pharmacy associations and to nurses and residents in medical schools and hospitals. The other is a group of physicians, paid by the company on a fee basis, who share their clinical experiences with these groups and groups of physicians. While neither group of speakers is directly selling SmithKline products, both are an important part of its marketing and sales effort.

Barb Schwarz, motivational and sales-training speaker from the Seattle area, has developed a sophisticated approach to sponsored speaking. She asks herself, what business might profit from exposure to the same target market I am addressing? If I want to expand my sales-training seminar into the real estate field, for example, would a cellular telephone company be interested in helping me get in front of those people? The answer is likely to be yes. Real estate salespeople who spend a great deal of time in their cars or walking around vacant property need to be in touch with their home offices. If I am doing customer service seminars for an association of travel agents, she asks, would an airline or a tourist bus company be interested in sponsoring my seminar? The possibilities are almost endless. Schwarz writes, "Using sponsors simply works. Try it. Jump in with both feet, and you'll be amazed at how easy it is . . . There are a lot of wonderful possibilities that will come your way when you start using sponsors."[5]

Trade associations also sponsor speakers, not for direct financial gain but to enhance the public's understanding of their members' work, to boost the image of an area, to improve the health of a population segment, or simply to enhance goodwill for the trade. A prime example is the Ohio Apple Marketers, who sponsor full-time speaker Steve Newman. As a young journalist, Newman spent four years walking around the world and relaying his informative and witty dispatches to the *Columbus Dispatch* and *Capper's*. As a kind of Ohio folk hero himself, whose books became widely read in Ohio schools, he identifies himself with Johnny Appleseed. The apple marketers pay him a fee plus expenses to speak to two schools a day, weaving the Johnny Appleseed stories with his own adventures to convey messages about morality, self-esteem, and other virtues.

My talks are sponsored by companies who want their names to be known by association with a reputable professional. When I give a talk on nutrition and fitness, my responsibility is to educate and motivate the audience. It's not necessary for me to keep mentioning my sponsor because the audience will become annoyed, stop listening, and I will lose my credibility. I want sponsors to feel they received more than they paid for, so I encourage acknowledgment of the sponsor

- in the meeting notice
- on the program
- on posters
- with product displays
- with brochures or coupons

- on handouts
- sometimes in a small logo on the slides
- with public thanks by the moderator
- with thanks again in an article about the talk in the client's newsletter, even if I have to write it myself.

In South Africa, Canada, Britain, and the United States, I have been sponsored by companies such as Kellogg's, Uncle Ben's Rice, Mead Johnson, Ross Products, McDonald's, and Baxter Healthcare Corporation. The talks may be held at various locations—conference centers, health shows, or association meetings. The topic often relates to the sponsor's products or services, but not always.

My book, *Feel Fantastic,* published by Macmillan Canada, has made sponsorship easier. One of my colleagues has organized a series of talks in Canada, receiving sponsorship from the teachers, dietetics, nurses, and recreational leaders associations and the Minister of Culture, Tourism, and Recreation. The package included eight talks, television tapings, moderating a fashion show, and book signings.

If you want your talks to be sponsored, you need to build a good reputation by

- becoming a leader in your field
- making a name for yourself in the media
- becoming known among your colleagues
- volunteering in your professional association
- becoming a media personality
- publishing many articles
- writing a book

Sponsored talks can increase your number of speaking engagements rapidly. Even if you have to approach numerous companies in the beginning, they will use you regularly once they start working with you.

Maye Musk is a lifestyle motivational speaker from San Francisco who holds two master of science degrees from South Africa and Canada and is a registered dietitian. She has served as president of the Consulting Dietitians of Canada and Southern Africa.

TODAY'S CHANGING PLATFORM

The lure of the platform to speakers and of audiences to people has always governed the chemistry between speaker and audience. That dynamic is not likely to change. Technology, however, is changing the relationship between speakers and audiences. The change is not at all to diminish or demean the speaker–audience dynamic but to enhance it.

Next to desktop projectors linked to notebook computers, the most obvious change is the wide-screen projection of the speaker's image—usually 25 feet square and well above the speaker in venues that attract audiences in the thousands. Theoretically, there is no audience too large for a speaker if there are enough screens and projectors available. Also, speakers can project onto those screens images from slides they bring or receive from a remote location, including the Internet. Teleconferencing equipment can enable a speaker—or even audience members—to interact with a business leader several thousand miles away.

Speakers who are also trainers are learning to utilize distance learning technology, now spawning a whole new industry. Students may take college courses by watching lecturers on cable or satellite, sending in their homework and taking examinations by e-mail. Alternatively, they may receive information on videotape or CD-ROM. Or they may use a hypertext-linked online video textbook that is keyed to audio and video sources crosslinked to any number of databases or other literature.

A simpler change is audiences' desire to "take the speaker home" in the form of audio- and videotapes. Using high-speed duplicating machines, audio cassettes can be made available minutes after the presentation. Video duplicates take longer, but orders can be filled in a day or two. Some speakers use their presentations to market an audiotape newsletter. A somewhat different spin is used by Robert Fish of California, who uses storytelling extensively in his presentations and has developed a subscriber base to *Fish Tales*, geared specifically for listening to stories on a cassette player while traveling in the car.

WHAT DOES IT TAKE TO MAKE YOUR LIVING AS A PROFESSIONAL SPEAKER?

Personal Characteristics

Becoming a full-time, professional speaker is an exciting, challenging process. It takes the best that is in anyone. Certainly it requires a high degree of rhetorical skill, but it also calls for the character and personality elements that are required of any successful speaker. Because of the highly competitive nature of the business, it requires assertiveness, patience, a passion for the subject, a strong and healthy ego, and a mature perspective that can cope with the time it takes to develop a successful business.

Self-Reflection

Self-reflection is the first step. Ask yourself: Is making my living on the platform something I must absolutely do to be fulfilled? Many an actor, painter, musician, athlete, and other kind of performer has faced the same question. Part of the question is whether you have an ego healthy enough to handle the inevitable rejection that will come when you offer your services to enough people. The other part is whether you have the discipline to manage your time and your resources to get you where you want to go. The challenges are so great that you must possess a deep conviction that it is the one thing in life you absolutely must do.

Many speakers have been helped by working with Juanelle Teague of Dallas, Texas, whose program "Specialize or Die" helps speakers to work through their personal belief systems as a prerequisite to careers on the platform. She leads her clients through a process of exploring their belief systems that she defines as "the foundation of your life experiences coming from family and key institutions that have impacted you from birth to your current age." From this analysis arise some keen insights as to where they will derive the energy they need and how they will function at their best. She asks them to rank in order of importance a list of about 30 values, such as money, recognition, security, excitement, service, productivity, competition, knowledge, and peace, to discover how congruent they are with a speaking career.

Subject Matter Expertise

Become very clear about your relationship with your subject. If you are an expert in a field for which you have been prepared by education and experience and are passionate about it, you needn't exercise much concern. However, many people enter the speaking business out of their own need to excel on a platform. They are in love with the very process of dazzling an audience, giving only a secondary regard to the information shared. Their first task is to make sure that their urge to speak is not a neurotic one, because if it is, they will not last long in the business. The second is to work hard at determining what they will talk about and to commit themselves to a high level of expertise. People who both love to speak and immerse themselves in their subjects enjoy a high degree of success.

While it is possible to build a profitable speaking business on an arbitrarily chosen topic, the effectiveness, comfort level, and longevity of the enterprise is far greater when the speaker has and conveys a genuine passion and involvement in the subject. It is one thing to collect and organize a lot of fine material on the global economy, technology, productivity, or some other popular topic; it is quite another to speak out of a deep reservoir of information, a keenly felt commitment to that topic, and the growing experience that continually enriches the presentations.

A Clear Statement of Your Mission

Knowing the destination has always been indispensable for people moving from one place to another. Today, increasing numbers of businesses are discovering the importance of articulating where they are going. Especially since the publication of Stephen Covey's book, *Seven Habits of Highly Effective People,* corporate boards, individual practitioners, and trade associations have invested enormous amounts of energy in the writing of mission statements.

Making a living as a speaker is just as much of a business as Microsoft or a hardware store—just smaller in scale. Adopting a mission statement both gives direction to the expenditure of energy and money and serves as a measure of how effective that spending is. A mission statement deals with four basic human needs: economic or money need, social or relationship need, psychological or growth need, and spiritual or contribution need. For example, a mission statement for a speaker whose primary topic is team leadership might aim for "a consistently profitable speaking business that enables corporate employees to develop the quality of relationships that will grow their business to its optimum size, contributing to the enrichment of their communities." A humorist will develop a very different mission, as will a speaker on foreign policy, parenting, accounting, personal growth, or negotiation skills.

A mission statement has to be dynamic and flexible to adapt to changing situations. It also needs to take into account the variety possible in the speaker's business. One speaker may choose a single topic, another a wide variety. One speaker may begin with no intention of selling books and tapes only to discover that audiences demand them—and so do the increasing needs of a growing family. One speaker may find the speaking assignments declining and the training dates increasing—or vice versa—and will change the mission statement accordingly.

A Business Plan

Getting started as a professional speaker requires the steps described in some detail in the preceding chapter on avocational speaking. Attempting to make a living on the platform, however, requires a much more sophisticated business plan, especially in the area of marketing. If you are considering moving into speaking as a full-time income source, these are the areas to be investigated.

Time Frame

Most full-time speakers ease their way into the business. They remain avocational speakers until their speaking income comes close to meeting their financial needs, either moving their primary job to part-time or quitting the job and filling in the gap with savings. Others simply leave their job and plunge into marketing themselves as speakers, placing their faith in God or their own ability to be successful. A fortunate few live on the income from a trust fund, have inherited or saved money, or can draw on the resources of a friend or family member, including a spouse, until success comes.

The estimates differ as to how long the journey to full-time status takes. Speakers' estimates of a realistic time frame, however, cluster around two to five years. What good planning calls for is a critical mass of speaking engagements that provides the possibilities of enough referrals to sustain the momentum. No one can predict with any certainty just when that will happen.

What is important is that you have a firm, written, realistic plan that does not place in danger your obligation to support a family, pay a mortgage, and save for a rainy day. The other danger is that anxiety about your financial situation may subtly diminish the energy and creativity you need to develop your speech material and to market yourself vigorously.

Projected Income and Expenses

The best estimate of your income will come from the size of fees you are receiving as an avocational speaker and their frequency. If you are receiving $100 to $200 a speech a couple of times a month—as a pattern over time—you are certainly not ready to jump into a full-time commitment. On the other hand, if you are making half as much income from speaking as your primary job pays and you are in ever-greater demand, you may consider making the big move. You will rarely hear successful speakers talk about their failure to time this move wisely, but in unguarded moments some will tell you that they wish they had moved into full-time speaking more slowly.

The expenses of starting a full-time speaking business can kill the enterprise very quickly if the speaker's business and marketing priorities are skewed. Beginning speakers have been known to rent office space, hire staff, buy advertising, rent mailing lists, and print elaborate materials before they knew either how relatively unimportant these steps are or where the money would come from. One of the beauties of the speaking business is its low overhead in the process of getting underway.

Nearly all full-time speakers operate from their homes—even those who once rented expensive office space. One exception is those very few who may operate a training business large enough to require an office staff, space for instructors' offices, and even training rooms. Another is those who offer an extensive line of books and tapes and genuinely enjoy supervising employees and dealing with inventory, mailing, and tape-duplicating equipment. Most speakers have discovered that it is generally more cost effective to contract out such business services.

Another money-wasting expense for beginning speakers is an elaborate press kit with four-color brochures, videotapes, refrigerator magnets, plastic paper clips bearing your name, and other advertising specialties. There may come a time when one or more of these items will fill a particular marketing need, but not at the beginning.

Bob Bloch, a veteran speaker on marketing topics, takes a realistic view of a speaker's income and expenses in the article "Designing a Speaker's Viable Marketing Plan." He reminds readers to ask how much disposable income they need; how much one must pay for office, staff, and subcontractor overhead; how much must go into unreimbursed business expenses, office equipment and repair, software, miscellaneous expenses, a contingency fund, and taxes.

> Assuming that $100,000 is the absolute minimum for the above, and we can be booked 35 times a year, we must set our fees at a little more than $2,850 a day. On a 50-times-a-year booking schedule, the $2,000-a-day fee will suffice. If our full-day presentations are seven

> hours in length—and it takes approximately 11.5 hours on stage to pay for preparation, staff work, and travel time—then we can conclude that a seven-hour presentation actually takes 87.5 hours. By dividing the daily fee of $2,000 by the hours required shows us that our gross pay is actually $22.85 an hour—less taxes and FICA, only approximately $13.71 an hour. Will we get rich on that amount? Probably not. [While] the average worker spends 2,000 hours on the job each year . . . with 50 presentations, we will have to use up 4,375 hours of our time . . . Is it worth it? You bet it is! My only regret is that I spent the first 42 years of my life not knowing about this wonderful opportunity.[6]

Other speakers will figure their income and expenses in very different ways, varying the number of preparation hours, the size of their fees, the number of dates they expect to be on the road, and the amount of their overhead. More important than the numbers is the process of making realistic financial projections.

Marketing

One definition of marketing is that it is anything and everything a person in business does to earn money—from putting on image-enhancing clothing every morning to sending a thank-you note to your customer after the speaking engagement. While there is some truth in that broad definition, it is less than practical for a speaker who is developing a plan that will lead to success. A more helpful way to working out a marketing plan is to move through three steps: positioning, contacting, and closing. *Positioning* involves doing those things that establish your credibility; *contacting* is doing the things that put you in front of the prospective buyer of your speaking talent; *closing* is getting an agreement to speak—perhaps an oral understanding, a handshake, or preferably a written and signed contract.

Positioning

The degree to which you will be hired and the amount of money you make depends a great deal on the perception meeting planners have of you. If you are a certified industry expert as well as an outstanding speaker, your route to speaking success is significantly enhanced. If you are speaking on a generic business topic like customer service, sales, or leadership, your verifiable experience in either or both will have a critical effect on your position in the marketplace.

A Niche Market. Many speakers have developed a niche market, a limited market usually thought of as targeted to an industry or profession. The industry expert has a natural niche market—the accounting expert speaking to groups of CPAs, the retired railroad executive speaking to transportation industry groups, the warehousing company manager speaking to manufacturers. Schools are a niche market, whether primary, secondary, or college. So also are women's groups, religious gatherings, chiropractors—indeed, any group with a common interest. Even if the speaker has no official connection to that market but offers a depth of information and insight to those audiences, a niche market exists for that speaker.

With little or no experience in real estate, dentistry, high technology, or another field, some extremely successful speakers have created a niche market for themselves. They have researched an industry of their choice with determination and skill because they have sensed a need there. They may have started with a speech to one local association or company in that field, perhaps by accident, and leveraged that experience into a profitable career. If a speaker is neither an industry expert nor well-begun in a business category, a choice can be made—but not arbitrarily. Juanelle Teague has developed an Industry Research System that takes clients through a detailed process by which they identify a specialized market and begin developing it as their own niche. They identify key people in a particular industry who can test-market that client's marketing efforts. They interview people in the targeted industry to determine major industry problems, work with them to explore possible solutions to those problems, study industry publications, form an alliance with industry leaders, and offer a free pilot program as a way to get started.

A niche market may also be limited to a geographic area. Steve Newman, earlier mentioned as a sponsored speaker, has developed his niche market as the state of Ohio, and particularly its schools. He has used his skill in telling the stories of Johnny Appleseed, one of Ohio's folk heroes, to develop a profitable speaking business, enhancing his income with books and tapes. About 90 percent of his speaking engagements are in Ohio, allowing him to book more billable days than speakers who must travel widely.

Authorship. Meeting planners are almost invariably attracted to authors in their search for a speaker. Fortunately for speakers, it doesn't seem to matter to them that the speaker's book is not a best seller or that it was not issued by a major publisher. Nor are meeting planners guaranteed to be readers of the book whose author they select as a speaker. A considerable industry, therefore, has developed for speakers who wish to publish a book. Nearly every issue of *Sharing Ideas* and *Professional Speaker* advertises companies that will help speakers to write, publish, and market a book, and every NSA convention exhibition hall features booths for self-publishing companies. Ghost writers are available for speakers whose writing skills are limited or who haven't found time to write. Graphic designers will subcontract to design the cover or the interior of the book. Some companies will only manufacture the book; others will manufacture and distribute it. All will consult with speakers on the process, offering whatever specialized service is needed. The primary value of authorship to beginning speakers lies in the very existence of a credible book, not the amount of money to be made from royalties. Even if the speaker contracts with a major publisher in the expectation of making a large profit in dollars, the speaker-author must still take a heavy responsibility to market the book through back-of-the-room sales, pre-seminar agreements, or direct marketing. Many authors contract for extra copies of the book's cover as a part of their press kit.

A full-length book is not the only print mode for enhancing one's position in the speaker market. Many speakers publish newsletters especially geared to their niche market. If they can develop insider or cutting-edge information on a regular basis from high-level, dependable sources whom they have cultivated, they are well poised for speaking engagements. Other speakers publish a series of short booklets on their subject, offered by direct mail marketing, as a fax-on-demand, or by advertising through an online service. One of the easiest and most popular ways to get into print is to write a column for a local newspaper or a business-oriented periodical. Good, up-to-date content written in a readable style, combined with a predictable, on-time delivery is attractive to many a busy editor and is a marvelous marketing opportunity for a speaker.

Acknowledged Expertise. If you are a speaker, you are an expert on something. Seize every opportunity to share your knowledge with the public. If you are attuned to news items about situations to which you can make an important contribution, you will receive recognition as an expert. If, for example, the media are highlighting the story of someone who has a nervous breakdown at the mall or a police officer who beats his wife, and you are a psychologist who specializes in stress-related problems, call the media and offer your expertise. If you are an environmentalist, call the media whenever a story appears about toxins in landfills, chemical water pollution, or waste seepage. Offer your expert comment on a celebrity divorce case if you are a lawyer with experience in family law. When you do, you are doing a favor both for some editor and for yourself. What is most important is that you call immediately when you sense the opportunity. If your expertise is used, place a thank-you call to the editor, remembering that the relationship you develop may well reverse the process, resulting in a call to you the next time your expertise is needed.

The print media may welcome you as a columnist and a broadcast reporter may welcome your expert comment on a news event if you go after those opportunities. So also may a radio or television program manager welcome you as a host for a regular program that conveys important information to the public, directly or through interviews with guests. The competition is stiff for this kind of air time, but the potential rewards for your availability are almost beyond calculation.

Press Kit. One important means of obtaining publicity is by a press kit that contains a variety of information about the speaker. While a well-organized press kit can never substitute for a strong, positive reputation as an outstanding speaker, it is nevertheless an important component in a speaker's positioning. It can be sent as a complete unit to inquirers who want to explore a speaker's credibility and to see a list of speech topics, or pieces of it can be provided for specific needs. It can also become a "backgrounder" for a program's master of ceremonies, a reporter, an editor, or a talk show host.

The ideal press kit includes the following:

1. A one-pager that includes basic information about you and your presentations: name, address, phone number, fax number, e-mail address, title and very brief theme of each speech, along with your qualifications. Extremely useful are commendations from clients and your picture. It should be professionally designed and printed in faxable black and white. This piece is the one indispensable item. See Appendix N for an excellent example.
2. A creative brochure, printed in color, with detailed information about yourself and your topics; more client letters; and additional services you offer, such as training seminars, consulting services, books, and tapes.
3. A detailed biography, indicating your educational achievements, industry background, speaking experience, and, if important and appealing, your family, civic or military involvement, hobbies, and anything else meeting planners might respond to favorably.
4. Copies of actual letters of endorsements by people who have heard you.
5. Glossy photograph of yourself—head and shoulders or an action shot.
6. Reprints of articles you have written on your topic.
7. Reprints of articles written *about* you.
8. Your newsletter, if you publish one.
9. List of products you offer: books and tapes.
10. Tapes—audio and/or video—of your actual presentations.
11. Fee schedule, sent on request only.
12. Boilerplate publicity release, announcing your appearance, with date, place, and sponsor name left open.
13. Cover letter—always customized.

Consistency. If publicity is to serve your speaking business well, it must be continuous. One or two press releases at the beginning of your career will do little or nothing for you.

Publicity simply does not generate itself; it requires constant attention. One of the best reasons for niche marketing is to be able to limit and intensify your ongoing publicity efforts. If you speak in a state, region, or a metropolitan area around a large city, you can develop media contacts with a reasonable number of editors, reporters, talk show hosts, corporate and Chamber of Commerce communication directors, and others who can keep your name in the news. If you major in an industry of any size, you can keep in contact with trade publication editors, newsletter producers, corporate communication people, and others who will print your articles, invite you to appear on radio/television panels, and otherwise make your presence known in that industry. If, on the other hand, you speak anywhere on any topic, you have an extremely difficult, though not totally impossible, public relations job.

Media Exposure. The indispensable tool of any publicity campaign is a well-researched media list, with accurate names and titles, to which you will send a frequent flow of information to keep your name in peoples' minds. Identify the radio and television stations along with the shows most likely to be interested in your topic. List the newspaper reporters and editors who can use material from you and about you. Be sure to include the trade press, consumer magazines, the general business media, syndicated business columnists, and Sunday newspaper supplements. Learn from each source what their interests are and what deadlines you must deal with. Sometimes your client can arrange for media appearances, but only if you are speaking in a distant location in which you have no media contacts. In general, the responsibility for media relations is yours.

Some exposure to the media can be purchased through an agent or a public relations company. If you can find a competent retired or unemployed public relations professional who will work for a modest fee, you are most fortunate. The average fee for a general PR firm to represent you runs between $1,500 and $2,500 a month plus expenses, based on the agency's hourly fee—with no guarantee that you will be placed. Some speakers hire an employee to do marketing—usually on an hourly basis—much of which involves generating publicity. These employees can do an excellent job of issuing news releases but seldom bring with them the contacts or the skill to open doors to media exposure.

Specialized media relations firms have recently been formed exclusively to place speakers and authors in contact with journalists and talk show producers, generally on a fee basis. These performance-based companies charge in the range of between $300 to book you on a local radio talk show to $6,000 for national television exposure on a show like the "Today" show or "Larry King Live." If you are expert on some topic of current news interest or have written a book, the chance of getting on a popular show is considerably enhanced. Media Relations of Minneapolis has been singularly successful in placing speakers who are also authors. You will find a list of some firms that supply assistance to speakers seeking publicity in Appendix H. An excellent printed resource, among many useful books on publicity, is *You Can Hype Anything* by Raleigh Pinsky (Citadel Press).

Internet. An increasing number of speakers report success from using the Internet. Some have used inexpensive software to create their own web pages. Other speakers develop their own web sites with the help of an online consulting company. Creating a web page with panache and getting your web address to the people you want to access your information is a big challenge. Subscribing to an online speaker marketing service seems to make sense for most full-time speakers. The Expertise Center exemplifies a widely used professional service designed to get speakers online. Operated by NSA members, it provides web-site development and access to meeting planners who are looking for speakers. Some online services enable potential buyers to view a segment of your audio- and videotapes and to provide a link to articles you have written, your schedule of speaking dates, a copy of your newsletter, and other data you may wish to provide. Several of these service providers are listed in Appendix G.

Being on the web is not magic: you still have the responsibility to let your clients and potential clients know where to find you on the web. Web-site marketing, therefore, is strictly supplementary to the referrals you earn and the print pieces you distribute.

Advertising. Paying for space in one of the directories of experts is a comparatively inexpensive way to make known your availability. A number of companies have arisen in recent years to provide listings of experts for print journalists and talk show hosts who wish to interview them. One of the oldest and largest resources is *The Yearbook of Experts, Authorities, and Spokespersons,* issued to twenty thousand journalists. About fifteen hundred experts on various topics pay to be listed. The extensive, 200-page index system facilitates searching by topic, location, and organization. The publication's web site enables the users to see the expert's directory space and to link to that person's web site.

An alternative medium is the publication *Radio-TV Interview Report,* published by Bradley Communications of Lansdowne, Pennsylvania. Unlike the two-inch thick *Yearbook,* it is a 64- to 88-page periodical that is sent to four thousand talk show hosts three times each month. Many who purchase space in this publication report that they have had numerous inquiries for telephone interviews on their subjects, some of which are broadcast in large media markets. Information about both the *Yearbook* and the *Interview Report* appears in Appendix H.

The association market can be reached through advertising in one of the journals read by association executives, almost all of whom look for speakers from time to time and some of whom spend a great deal of money hiring them. Each year *Association Management,* published by the American Society of Association Executives, issues its *NSA/ASAE Guide to Using Professional Speakers* for its twenty-three thousand members. A prime example of a regional directory is *Western Association News,* whose readers work with associations throughout the western states and who are responsible for planning more than one hundred and fifty thousand off-site meetings every year. A list of state and regional associations is available from the American Society of Association Executives in Washington, D.C. Advertising in a trade show journal or an industry newsletter may have considerable value for speakers who are establishing their position in a particular niche.

Networking. Every technique that has been suggested for positioning is an arms-length technique. People can see your name in print or on a computer screen, hear you on the radio, or see you on television, but none of them begins to measure up to a face-to-face conversation with a person who may be in a position to hire you or to refer you. Every speaking engagement is an occasion for networking. The conversations before and after the meeting are filled with possibilities for more speaking dates. Many speakers have learned to grow their business by attending gatherings to mix and talk with people who can further their careers. At the local level, a Chamber of Commerce is a good place for networking contacts. Speakers in a niche market attend its association meetings. Local gatherings of Meeting Professionals International welcome speakers and trainers as vendor members.

Bureau Relationships. The previous chapter described the function of a speakers bureau as a broker between the meeting planner—whose interests the bureau represents—and the speaker, who pays the bureau a commission for obtaining the engagement. The speaker who cultivates a positive relationship with a bureau may experience a significant income through bookings that no amount of direct marketing from the speaker's office could generate. The bureau will present speakers' names to its clients if it has supreme confidence in the speaker's ability to deliver a first-class presentation and if the speaker works in a team relationship with the bureau. That relationship must be characterized by the highest ethical standards and by honoring the bureau's policies and procedures.

Your primary positioning tool is your reputation as a superb speaker. If your material is well researched, your stories fresh and creative, your delivery highly polished, and your human relationships considerate and ethical, the referrals you will get from the excellence of your work will earn you bookings that no high-priced press kit, no telephone marketing campaign, no advertising, no direct mail program can possibly bring you. In addition, the publicity you receive, properly generated and handled, will always be a high-priority marketing tool, helping to keep your income and marketing expenses in profitable balance.

Contacting

Once you are firmly established by positioning as a credible person who speaks well, your job is to be considered by a person or a committee charged with finding a speaker for an engagement. You will use many of the tools of positioning to get on the list, some of them persuasive enough to take you straight through the contacting and closing steps for a particular speaking job. The long view of building a profitable speaking business, however, requires a more systematic marketing program that will consistently make contact with the decision makers who can keep your schedule full. You will find several sources for identifying meeting planners in Appendix E.

Discovering who makes the decision to hire a speaker is seldom easy. It is a task loaded with uncertainty and confusion for speakers at every level. People who hold the title of corporate meeting planner may occasionally be involved in hiring a speaker but are more likely to plan every other phase of a meeting—location, menu, seating, visual aid resources, and other logistical concerns. If the engagement you are seeking is a training seminar, a company's training manager might seem like the person to contact and sometimes it is. However, in many companies, training is contracted for by department heads who do not ask for help from the training people and sometimes do not even inform them that the training is taking place. One important place to look for the real decision maker is the line-of-business managers in the larger corporations who may take responsibility for meetings designed to increase their share of profitability, either in seminars or motivational meetings. In small to midsized companies, the CEO's secretary is a key person who calls speakers bureaus for suggestions to be passed on to the CEO. Sales managers themselves usually decide on a sales trainer or on a motivational speaker.

In a company with heavily decentralized management, employee task forces or quality circles may be given the responsibility to find a speaker. Vickie Sullivan, a marketing consultant to speakers, writes,

> Because speaker selection/training committees are fairly new in the corporate market, many of the committee

> members don't know anything about hiring speakers or trainers. Therefore, they build a linear process designed to remove the guesswork of selecting topics and vendors. Here is the most common procedure I've seen: develop an assessment tool, gather the results, report the results, choose the topics, develop the specs for vendors (sometimes this step is forgotten, making for some interesting proposals), examine the proposals, make the first cut, and then decide. Result: a drawn-out process with very little room for the most common marketing activity—persuasion over the telephone. Association committees are pros at using education committees, as they have been in place for years . . . It is the members, through the committees, that drive the selection process . . . Your effectiveness lies in your ability to influence others so they can influence others about you.[7]

The telephone is still the instrument of choice for contacting prospects. With the omnipresence of telephone answering machines, voice mail, and administrative assistants who act as gatekeepers, getting through readily is difficult if not impossible. The best use of the phone is generally to make an appointment for a phone conversation. Another method of contacting is e-mail, a method many speakers are finding successful for getting that coveted phone appointment. One professional speaker sends a follow-up letter to prospects who don't return calls with a few simple questions about event dates and times. He asks the prospect to write his or her answers on the letter and return it. Joe Bonura, president of a training company, faxed a questionnaire to a prospect with a request for completion and a telephone appointment to discuss it. In one instance the prospect returned the questionnaire by mail and included a company press kit. Bonura writes, "They hired me for four days of training. He later said he appreciated that we cared enough to learn about his business before making recommendations. He hired me in the end because we requested a telephone appointment, which was professional and respected his time."[8]

One reality to contend with is that the typical corporate or association meeting planner has a significantly different mindset from the speaker. The decision maker, almost always an employee, is by nature conservative—careful not to hire a speaker whose work is in any way unpredictable or threatening to the planner's status. That's why excellent positioning has to precede the contacting process. Conversations during the contacting process need to engage in the kind of questions and assurances that will help make the decision maker supremely comfortable with the decision.

Closing

The final phase of marketing is getting the meeting planner to say yes. The simple way of describing how a sale takes place is that all the variables are right for both parties. "Almost" doesn't do it.

If the positioning and marketing have been done skillfully, what remains are a few questions in the meeting planner's mind, sometimes expressed but often unexpressed. When the speaker is ready to deal with these questions, completing the arrangements is most likely to happen.

The meeting planner's first question is, Will this speaker achieve the meeting's goals? If the positioning and marketing efforts have done their job, the next question concerns the price. Presumably the positioning has put both the speaker and the planner in the same range. Whether you are in the $500 to $1,000 category or the $3,000 to $5,000 category, you must reach an agreement on the price. While some speakers claim they never deviate from their announced fee, most of them are willing to negotiate the best deal they can get. That negotiation may involve a lower fee if important decision makers will be in the audience or if they will speak at a second convention gathering for less than the total of two standard fees. A motivational speaker may, for example, be willing to lead a breakout session at no additional charge if the announced fee is accepted. The negotiation may involve changing the speaking fee if back-of-the-room sale of books and tapes is permitted or if workbooks or tapes are supplied to each participant. If the speaker is a qualified consultant in an area where the corporation or association needs help, some arrangement can generally be developed to the mutual satisfaction of speaker and planner. When the planner wants the speaker and the speaker wants the engagement, creativity can generally close the gap.

When I was dean of adult and continuing education at Tusculum College in Tennessee, a friend of mine, who was a colleague at another small college, called me one day and said, "We're looking for a keynote speaker. We'd like someone to come and do something light and humorous, but have a clear focus on what we're missing in targeting new markets for small colleges." He knew that the program I was doing at Tusculum was really successful. We went from recruiting five hundred evening students looking for nontraditional degree programs to two thousand in about eight months. They wanted to know what we were doing. Essentially, it was people skills—little things, good customer service, phone calls to see how satisfied they were.

I thought, am I the right person to do this? I had been teaching forever but had never had the occasion to be up on a stage to do any type of presentation. I told him I'd think about it, and he said that would be OK except that my name was already on the program because he thought I'd be honored to do it! So I spent the next couple of weeks trying to get a handle on it. I had a ball—a lot of laughter. Someone came up to me afterwards—an NSA member—and asked how long I had been speaking professionally. I said, "About 48 minutes."

People began calling me, and about six weeks later I got my first speaking date with Disney. At that first meeting they asked me what I charged, and I said whatever their honorarium is would be OK. I was shocked when I got a check for $2,500. And I thought, 45 minutes for $2,500—almost a month's salary! This could be me! And it went from that! I had a tremendous first year as a full-time speaker.

M. Dale Henry, speaker, is principal of Your Best Unlimited of Kingston, Tennessee.

NOTES

1. Robert Johnson, "For One Reagan You Can Get Many Mikki Williamses," *The Wall Street Journal,* January 30, 1992, p. 1.
2. Robin S. Sharma, "The Future of Work: Spirituality in the Boardroom," *Sharing Ideas,* October/November 1996, p. 10.
3. John Alston, "Topic Development," *Professional Speaker,* October 1996, p. 4.
4. Steven Seligman, "Non-Academic Learning for Busy Adults," *Sharing Ideas,* Fall 1996, p. 9.
5. Barb Schwarz, "Using Sponsors to Increase Your Speaking Business," *Professional Speaker,* May 1995, p. 36.
6. Bob Bloch, "Designing a Speaker's Viable Marketing Plan," *Professional Speaker,* September 1995, p. 30.
7. Vickie Sullivan, "Who's on First: Selling Your Programs to Education Committees," *Professional Speaker,* May 1995, p. 12.
8. Joe Bonura, "Four Creative Selling Ideas from an Ad Man Turned Speaker," *Professional Speaker,* September 1996, p. 28.

The Speaking Industry

Many people observing the speaking business are aware only of speakers in front of audiences. To view only those two participants would be like seeing the health-care industry solely in terms of doctors treating patients. Everyone knows that the relationship between doctors and patients could not occur apart from a complex system of people and institutions that contribute to the healing process: hospitals with their large staffs of administrators, technicians, nurses, and maintenance people; health insurance companies; suppliers of surgical kits, linens, and food services. Like physicians, speakers may be the most important players in the speaking business—the ones most visible to the public eye. Like physicians, they generally—but not always—make more money than most of the people who support their endeavors. But they could not function without the aid of a great many people and institutions who are neither on the platform nor in the audience. The growth of professional speaking during the last quarter century has produced an assemblage of companies, associations, and consultants large enough to be called an industry—the speaking industry.

To round out the story of public speaking in our society, especially in its business dimensions, requires a careful look at the people and institutions that have grown up around the phenomenon of a speaker talking to an audience—people whose livelihoods derive from that speaker–audience interaction. Without the phenomenon of a speaker addressing an audience, many people who now make the speaker's job easier or more productive would not be in business. This chapter will attempt to delineate each of these supporting roles and indicate at least some of the varieties in each. Not included are businesses such as print shops, attorneys, computer resellers, accountants, and merchants of office furniture—all of whom profit because speakers and trainers by the tens of thousands face audiences every day. Surely someone will some day calculate the economic impact of the speaking industry on U.S. society and find it to be huge.

You have come this far in the book because you are interested, for reasons of your own, in exploring the meaning of public speaking for yourself. You may be a Toastmaster intrigued by the possibility of making some money with your stand-up communication skills, a graduate student who wants to become a motivational speaker, a downsized executive looking for a new livelihood, a psychotherapist wanting to become better known in the community as a means of extending your practice. Help is available to you through a small but vital industry geared to your needs. If you are an experienced, professional speaker—avocational or full-time—you may become aware in this chapter of the vast array of help available for ensuring your continued success.

You may, also for reasons of your own, wish to contribute to the phenomenon of public speaking without preparing and presenting speeches. The following material may open an even wider set of options, making you aware of just how many ways you can be involved in the public speaking industry, even if you never mount a platform. Many of the elements of the industry listed here have been touched on throughout the book. This chapter's purpose is to group the elements of the business in one place, making sure that each is understood in light of the whole.

SPEAKERS BUREAUS

The proliferation of speakers bureaus in the last couple of decades is astounding. More than five hundred bureaus have been formed in the United States since the mid-1970s, when the number could be counted on the fingers of one hand. In addition, the bimonthly magazine *Sharing Ideas* lists a half-dozen new bureaus in each issue. The most rapid growth is occurring in other countries, 16 of which now boast bureaus. Most of them are in Canada, Australia, England, and other English-speaking countries—but increasing numbers are appearing in other parts of the world. Sweden, Taiwan, and Venezuela each have a speakers bureau. *Sharing Ideas* publishes the only up-to-date listing of bureaus, available on special order (see the listing in Appendix B under Magazines/Periodicals for Speakers).

Association with one of these bureaus—sometimes called lecture bureaus—is a way for nonspeakers to become involved in the speaking industry. The larger bureaus employ general agents and those who specialize in celebrities or college circuit speakers. Recent college graduates who have participated in the booking of college events are especially useful in marketing speakers for the college market. The larger bureaus employ marketing and financial staff as well as clerical support persons for the day-to-day operation of the business.

The more likely route to involvement in the bureau business, since there is only a handful of fully staffed bureaus, is to start your own. Many beginners have learned the business by consulting with those who are successful and starting out on their own. They accelerate their progress by joining the bureaus' trade association, the International Group of Agencies and Bureaus. Others have significantly shortened their learning curve by listening to a set of tapes, *How to Start and Build a Successful Speakers Bureau,* by Dottie Walters and Somers White, produced by Royal Publishing of Glendora, California. If you are already a successful speaker, you may wish to join the handful of speakers who have formed speakers bureaus of their own as additional profit centers for their speaking businesses. They already know how bureaus operate and can utilize many years of contacts they have developed in the industry, including both meeting planners and other speakers. One example of this phenomenon is Fran Tarkenton, former football star, who is both a motivational speaker and the owner of a speakers bureau.

General Business Bureaus

General business bureaus, sometimes called full-service bureaus, book speakers on any topic for any audience. Some lean toward serving a particular region, industry, or profession, but they are basically generalists. They may fill a client's request from their file of available speakers or they may work with other bureaus to find just the right speaker through an arrangement called co-brokering. Examples of general bureaus are Five Star Speakers and Trainers in the Kansas City area, Charisma Productions in Indianapolis, Speaker Services in Springfield, Pennsylvania, Speakers Guild in Sandwich, Massachusetts, and Standing Ovations in San Diego. Bureaus generally charge speakers 20 percent to 30 percent of their fees.

Celebrity Bureaus

Like the Redpath organization that booked Charles Dickens, Mark Twain, and others, many bureaus either book only celebrities or major in celebrity bookings. The Washington Speakers Bureau, for example, works with only 30 nationally known, high-fee speakers whom they represent on an exclusive basis. The Harry Walker Agency and the Greater Talent Network in New York and the American Program Bureau in Boston specialize in high-profile speakers and major entertainment figures. Keppler Associates in the metropolitan Washington, D.C., area represents several nationally known celebrities but also offers business speakers and lecturers for the college market. Even some much smaller bureaus handle celebrities, such as the Entertainment Alliance of California.

Targeted Market Bureaus

Just as some speakers have concentrated on niche markets, so have new bureaus arisen to service special markets. Advantage International in the Washington area works only with athletes and coaches who present inspirational messages. Admire Presentations, near New York City, provides only for college audiences. Patton Consultant Services of Boston limits its business to nonprofit groups. Contemporary Forum of Chicago books only authors and poets. Dammah Productions of New London, Connecticut, books minority and ethnic speakers. Class Speakers in San Marcos, California, specializes in Christian speakers for church gatherings. Gay and lesbian speakers are available through Out on the Podium of Los Angeles. The Agricultural/Professional Speakers Network of Zionsville, Indiana, services the agribusiness industry. Cruise ship bookings are the target of CTI Recruiting and Placement Agency of Ft. Lauderdale, Florida, and Creative Cruises Exclusively in Sterling Heights, Michigan.

This description of targeted market bureaus may suggest yet another area of opportunity for someone who wishes to take the chance of entering this increasingly competitive field.

SPEAKERS' REPRESENTATIVES

Speakers are sometimes represented by persons who can facilitate their business and free them from marketing efforts. These representatives are of two kinds: agents and managers.

Celebrities generally have their *agents* handle the speaking engagements that come to them. The celebrity may have a personal agent or employ a firm that represents several celebrities to negotiate contracts with a sports franchise, a publisher, or a television network and to handle speaking engagements. Other celebrities may, on the other hand, entrust those activities to an attorney who handles such matters. Generally, the agent receives 10 percent to 15 percent of each speaking fee.

Full-time speakers who have heavy speaking schedules and charge high enough fees may employ salaried *managers* or marketing associates who earn commissions. They almost always work in the speaker's office but sometimes out of their own home offices. A common pattern involves a speaker's spouse as marketer/manager. These managers not only market the speaker but facilitate the scheduling and transportation arrangements and handle the correspondence that precedes and follows many appearances. When the production and sale of books and tapes becomes an important part of the speaker's cash flow, the manager may work with a printer or tape producer, fill orders personally, or deal with a fulfillment company. The manager handles the innumerable details that come up in any business.

The number of people doing this work is large enough to support a professional emphasis group for speakers' staff members that meets at the NSA conventions and winter workshops. Persons who are content to stay in the background of the speaking industry and who have a good head for business can develop successful and rewarding careers representing speakers.

PUBLIC SEMINAR COMPANIES

Public seminar companies, discussed earlier, provide one- or two-day seminars in sizable metropolitan areas on topics of specialized interest. The one-day cost to participants is quite low, and the number of persons present is generally large. Both avocational and full-time speakers provide the instruction, always using a standardized curriculum. A list of these companies appears in Appendix C.

In addition to the presenters, who function as independent contractors, each one of these companies engages a staff of persons who have developed expertise in a particular part of the business. The staff includes receptionists, bookkeepers, schedulers, marketing people, and managers. Some staff people write and design curriculum; some screen and help to fine-tune new presenters; others handle the registrations and other daily operations, while yet others travel to monitor the quality of presentations.

MEETING PLANNERS

Meeting planner is a broad term that includes people who plan the convention menus and assign the rooms, the student chair of the college lecture committee, and the corporate CEO who decides which speaker will give the convention's keynote address.

Executives of associations and corporations are the most likely to make decisions about hiring speakers. Which executive depends on the size and complexity of the operation. In many trade associations, the executive director recommends one or more speakers to the board or a convention committee. The group may take the executive's advice, may ask to see one or more videotapes or may offer more names. If a corporation is large enough, one manager of a line of business such as operations, sales and marketing, or research and development may make the decision. Colleges and universities follow a wide variety of decision-making procedures that involve various combinations of students and staff members, making marketing to them a challenging task for speakers.

While not many people give all their time to hiring speakers, the role of hiring and scheduling speakers is an important one. Many people within corporations and associations and on college campuses spend considerable time and energy contributing to the health of their operations by choosing speakers and trainers.

ASSOCIATIONS

One of the most universal human tendencies is to gather with persons who share the same interests. Speakers and people in the speaking industry are no exception. Sometimes gatherings of speakers are small and informal and are held in someone's home or board room. Other times they involve people by the thousands meeting in a convention hotel. Several associations have grown out of the speaking industry. Two of them, the National Speakers Association and Toastmasters International, have been discussed at some length already and are listed here with a brief description for the sake of completeness. Information about reaching these and other speaker organizations appears in Appendix A.

National Speakers Association (NSA)

In 1973, a small group of speakers gathered under the leadership of Cavett Robert and Merlyn Cundiff to form an association to advance their work as platform speakers and to promote high ethical standards for its members. They had been sponsoring sales seminars in Phoenix since 1969. Many of the members were beginning to sense a need for a more responsible and professional movement. Starting with entertaining and motivational topics only, NSA members began to move toward meeting industry's demands for educational topics. From a membership of a few dozen core members and 189 people at its first convention at Phoenix in 1975, membership has grown to more than thirty-seven hundred persons, with around two thousand attending annual conventions. The national staff, headquartered at Tempe, Arizona, performs the usual functions of an association: keeping track of members, publishing promotional and educational materials, handling the funds, providing liaison with state and regional chapters, planning annual meetings, and responding to the questions and needs of its members. In addition, the NSA staff services the association's International Center for Professional Speaking, which offers several workshops throughout the year and provides online services to members.

All 37 chapters of the NSA are run by members who serve as officers. Some of the larger ones, however, employ managers who handle the membership details—registrations for meetings, reservations with the hotel or other venue, maintenance of the mailing list, promotion of special events such as a speakers school or a showcase, and the collection and expenditure of dues. One member may take on this responsibility for a fee or the chapter may hire an association management company, which adds the NSA chapter to the list of other small associations for which it performs similar duties.

Toastmasters International

Toastmasters arose out of the vision of one man, Ralph C. Smedley, a YMCA executive who formed the first club in 1903 as a youth activity in Bloomington, Illinois, where he was the Y's director of education. That club and those he started in the other towns to which he was transferred in the Midwest did not last. It was when he arrived at Santa Ana, California, in 1924 that the concept caught on with the optimistic, "let's try it" Californians. Toastmasters clubs sprang up in adjoining towns, and when the first club was formed in Canada in 1932, the movement became Toastmasters International.

The movement has grown to a worldwide membership of more than one hundred and seventy-one thousand people in more than eighty-two hundred clubs. A large, modern facility in Mission Viejo, California, contains a busy group of about sixty professionals and staff members who support the clubs with educational literature, badges and trophies of achievement, learning cassettes and videotapes, marketing services, a 32-page monthly magazine called *The Toastmaster,* and a listening ear for club challenges. A highly sophisticated computer system keeps track of the members who compete in the large number of area, division, district, and regional meetings and contests and whose participation earns them recognition.

Innumerable Toastmasters have moved on to positions of importance in business, government, and professional endeavors, having learned not only stand-up communication skills but also leadership skills, which they developed as officers in Toastmasters groups at various levels. Any sizable gathering of professional, full-time speakers would reveal a significant percentage of persons who began as Toastmasters.

Speech Communication Association (SCA)

Founded in 1914 as an association of speech teachers, the Speech Communication Association (SCA) is a national professional organization for scholars, researchers, teachers, and practitioners in various aspects of human communication. It is the oldest and largest national organization to promote communication scholarship and education—with members in every state and more than twenty foreign countries.

The association is composed of divisions that attract persons interested in such areas as rhetorical and communication theory, applied communication, public address, instructional development, and theatre. There are commissions for communication ethics, freedom of expression, and spiritual communication, among others. The SCA publishes six quarterly journals and a bulletin for high school and college communication instructors.

Each year, more than three thousand members gather for a four-day convention that consists largely of academic papers read in small groups to a wide variety of interests. Many affiliated organizations meet concurrently with the SCA annual meeting, such as the American Forensic Association and the Religious Speech Communication Association, which hold their business meetings and provide programs within the convention schedule and space. Like the other associations that serve the speaking industry, the SCA's national staff includes a mix of professionals—ex-professors and public school teachers—and support staff.

To make possible the participation of a larger number of people and to deal with local or regional issues, several state and regional associations meet throughout the country. Their structure and convention programs are similar to the national body.

American Society for Training and Development (ASTD)

The American Society for Training and Development (ASTD) celebrated its 50th birthday in 1994 as an organization with more than fifty-four thousand members, most of them affiliated with the national association but some involved only in local chapters. With the exception of some vendor members, all are involved in training. Represented in every industry group from accounting to utilities, trainers constitute the cutting edge of industrial and business growth. Corporate and government employees as well as independent trainers gather at the ASTD's national convention and in 168 chapters throughout the United States and Canada. The thrust of the organization may be seen best in its goals for the program called Vision 2000. It vowed that by the year 2000, it would

- lead new efforts to improve performance at work,
- find, create, and disseminate the world's most successful practices for achieving better performance at work,
- be a first source of information on workplace learning and performance,
- form partnerships with diverse individuals, organizations, and communities to improve workplace learning, and
- create opportunities for continual learning and professional development for itself as an organization and for its members.

Since a great deal of speakers' work fits into the category of training, many speakers belong to the ASTD, and many ASTD members—especially free-lancers—are members of the National Speakers Association.

National Association of Campus Activities (NACA)

The National Association of Campus Activities (NACA) came into being in 1969 to expedite cooperative bookings of entertainers on the college and university circuit. It soon began to add lecturers. In order for colleges to minimize their costs, NACA facilitates the arrangements by which several member institutions may cooperate on booking dates. One lecturer, rock band, juggler, hypnotist, or comedian may appear on subsequent days at several colleges in the same area, reducing the fees and travel costs to each college.

The association roughly parallels the much larger Association of Performing Arts Presenters, whose members deal exclusively with high-profile, high-fee engagements of groups such as symphony orchestras, international dance troupes, and theatrical productions.

One of NACA's chief functions is to sponsor an annual convention, plus several regional conventions, at which students and college staff members can audition and negotiate with presenters. It employs a staff of professionals and support persons in its national office in Columbia, South Carolina.

International Group of Agencies and Bureaus (IGAB)

An appropriate acronym for an organization concerned with people who talk for a living is IGAB, the trade association for speakers bureaus, headquartered in Indianapolis. The brainchild of Dottie Walters of Glendora, California, in the mid-1980s, it brought together a handful of persons who ran the country's speakers bureaus. Many were facing questions about ethical problems in the area of commissions, add-on fees, the holding of dates, contracts of exclusivity, and other matters. The group has since grown significantly, mirroring the increasing number of bureaus. It now conducts an annual showcase for speakers, facilitates cooperation in co-brokering speakers, and sponsors studies on the use of the Internet and other changes in the bureau business. It is managed by a professional association management firm in Indianapolis.

International Platform Association (IPA)

The primary activity of the International Platform Association (IPA) is its summer convention, always held in Washington, D.C. Speakers from both political parties, the college lecture circuit, and the business community address the participants. Founded in 1831 by Daniel Webster and Josiah Holbrook as the American Lyceum Association, the association draws several hundred people to its yearly event. It secures some of the country's most high-profile celebrities and balances them with less well-known speakers. A contest called the Speaking Ladder invites all comers to a competition that places the winner on the association's main program. A Speaking Seminar is offered with instruction on improving speaking skills, as is a storytelling workshop. The IPA's office in Winnetka, Illinois, is administered by a small staff.

PRODUCERS

Showcases

As the speaking industry has grown, so has the challenge for meeting planners to choose the right speakers for their meetings. Persons responsible for choosing speakers receive an abundance of brochures, tapes, and phone calls from speakers, their marketers, and speakers bureaus. If they consult with colleagues or other meeting planners, they can get conflicting opinions of a prospective speaker's worth. One kind of help they welcome is the opportunity to hear speakers in person.

To respond to this need, showcases have sprung up to which planners come to hear a variety of speakers, meet them in person, and negotiate speaking dates. Some are sponsored by speakers bureaus, others by NSA chapters. Some convene for half a day; others for an entire day. One of the oldest and largest bureau showcases is sponsored by Jordan International Enterprises in Roswell, Georgia. It set the pattern for a rapidly increasing number of these events. Speakers are usually asked to share the costs of marketing the event, and some ask planners for a modest registration fee, generally paid by the planners' companies or their associations. Similarly, NSA chapters invite meeting planners in their areas to showcases where chapter members can give a shortened version of one of their presentations and mingle with people they hope will hire them.

Rally/Seminars

Residents of major metropolitan areas are familiar with the intense marketing efforts that precede a gigantic, all-day motivational rally in a city's largest auditorium. Full-page newspaper ads, radio and television commercials, and direct mail campaigns to a variety of mailing lists promote attendance. Human resource executives are contacted to give discount vouchers to employees. High-profile speakers like Zig Ziglar, Robert Schuller, and General Norman Schwartzkopf join famous athletes and other celebrities to draw crowds that number in the thousands. Much of the payoff for the rally producer is obviously the "gate"—money paid for tickets—but the producer also receives a generous slice of the back-of-the-room sales of the speakers' books and tapes.

D. John Hammond of Scottsdale, Arizona, pioneered these rallies in the 1950s. Currently one of the nation's largest and most successful rally producers is Peter Lowe International of Tampa, which sponsors rallies throughout the United States. Attendance in 1996 rose 50 percent from the previous year—to a total of more than three hundred and eight thousand people. Peak Performers Network of Minneapolis brings a succession of prominent speakers to 10 major cities, providing seven evening programs a year in each city, each one preceded by an hour of networking. For a yearly subscription fee, usually split between a company and an employee, opportunity is given to hear such speakers as

Brian Tracy, Terry Bradshaw, and Les Brown. A similar, smaller company, Yes! A Positive Network, of Auburn Hills, Michigan, offers a Super Rally Seminar Series to more than five thousand members in Detroit, Cleveland, and Pittsburgh.

The very size of these seminars make entry into this side of the speaking business extremely difficult. Obtaining speakers with name recognition requires paying them high fees and therefore needing to attract a large attendance. Getting the critical mass of people, in turn, requires fairly modest entry fees. Promoters need to be extremely well capitalized, both to market the rallies and to assume the risk of bad weather, conflicting events, or unanticipated circumstances.

SPEECH WRITERS

Corporate speech writers are among the best-paid persons in the speaking industry. One reason is that many of them do their speech writing as heads of corporate communications departments in major industrial corporations or as high-level civilians in military or other government agencies. Very few persons are employed today to spend all their time and energy writing speeches. A typical description for a job that might interest a speech writer appeared in a newsletter read by speech writers. Submitted by a major corporation seeking a public relations manager, it sought someone to

> manage public relations programs; develop and implement strategic communications plans; establish relationships with news media and industry consultants to ensure positive and accurate reporting; develop and write speeches, video and demo scripts, and briefing materials; grant and manage interviews; and prepare spokespeople.

Some free-lance writers have developed a speech-writing business by cultivating relationships with corporate and government executives, especially in the corporate communications departments. Unfortunately, the downsizing of many large corporations has minimized the number of these people. However, there are enough corporate and independent speech writers in the Chicago area to form a vigorous Speech Writers Roundtable that meets monthly, alternating between the city and the suburbs. Similar groups meet in other major cities. The metropolitan Washington, D.C., area may have the most speech writers per capita because of the large number of government bodies, national association headquarters, and lobbying firms.

PERIODICALS

For Speakers

Three major publications are available to persons interested in the public speaking industry. One, *Professional Speaker*, is specifically targeted to people who make some or all of their living on the platform—dues-paying members of the National Speakers Association. It features topical articles by members and news of the association's members and activities. The second, *The Toastmaster*, is also for members of Toastmasters clubs, paid for as part of members' dues. The third is *Sharing Ideas*, produced by Royal Publishing in Glendora, California, for a wider variety of people—speakers and aspiring speakers—and also for vendors and persons with connections to the speaking industry. It offers book and tape reviews, news of bureau activities, columns on cruise and international speaking, technology trends, and an extensive array of short and practical articles on speaking and the speaking industry.

Persons interested in writing about public speaking or the speaking industry are welcome to submit ideas and articles to any of these periodicals. In addition, there are hundreds of other periodicals that welcome feature articles, biographies, commentaries on contemporary speeches, and even manuscripts of speeches given in various venues. *Vital Speeches of the Day,* available in most public libraries, publishes speeches given by business and civic speakers. Further information about these periodicals and others appears in Appendix B.

For Speech Writers

Speech writers receive excellent ideas from one or both of the two publications to which they can subscribe. *The Speechwriter's Newsletter,* published semimonthly in Chicago by Ragan Communications, is subtitled "The Voice of the Silent Profession." It contains articles on the craft by speech writers and an idea file with highly useable anecdotes, statistics, humor, and quotations. *The Executive Speaker,* published in Dayton, Ohio, is a monthly whose strength is its insightful analysis of important sections of speeches delivered in the business community. It offers samples of openings, closings, and in-between materials. It also offers a supplement called "Resources," which reviews books, tapes, CDs, downloads, quotation services, and miscellaneous software packages of interest to speech writers. Complete manuscripts of all the speeches it excerpts are available on special order. While directed to professional speech writers, there is much of value to persons who are serious about the quality of their presentations—especially in the area of precise and evocative language.

RESOURCES FOR SPEAKERS

Books

Most bookstores have a good selection of books and tapes geared to help persons who have a speech to make. If you are online, the Internet provides an even wider selection of books and tapes on Amazon, "the world's largest bookstore," www.Amazon.com. The number and variety of these materials are staggering. Most of the titles provide step-by-step help for preparing and delivering speeches; the rest provide humor, quotations, and other materials for speeches. Another source is the direct mail providers who offer books and tapes to their lists. A few books written for persons who wish to enter the speaking business have been published. Most of the titles are now out of print but may be available through a used book source. A list of these is to be found in Appendix D.

As many as there are of these how-to books, there seems always to be room in the market for one more. If you have a unique approach to writing on the subject of speaking, the chances are good you can find an interested publisher.

Software

A smaller but growing category of help for speakers is software. One kind is the relatively straightforward presentation software that is built into word processors such as Microsoft Word and WordPerfect. Another is the targeted software, such as PowerPoint and Astound, that can produce sophisticated slides, overheads, and multimedia presentations.

A third kind of software aims to take the speaker through the process of creating a speech. "Interactive Speechwriter for Windows" (also available for Mac users), published by Allyn

& Bacon, is used in college classes in conjunction with the texts it accompanies. It is a menu-driven, user-friendly guide to composing a speech. More of this kind of software is being developed all the time.

MARKETING SERVICES

Online Services

In the mid-1990s, computer technology brought into the speaking industry an entirely new entity, an online marketing service for speakers and meeting planners. Among the early entrants were Wally Bock, Ken Braly, and Jeff Senne, all members of the National Speakers Association who knew firsthand a great deal about speakers' marketing needs. Others also formed companies to utilize the Internet, especially the World Wide Web, to provide an ideal meeting place for speakers and meeting planners. The approach of these companies is twofold: (1) to help speakers develop their own web pages, and/or (2) to develop proprietary web pages in which a number of speakers can list their topics, backgrounds, and words of applause from satisfied clients. As the technology improves, meeting planners are gaining access to the audio and video of the speakers' presentations. Some NSA chapters have developed their own web pages for the benefit of their members. A listing of some of the online service providers is in Appendix G.

How many of these providers can enter the marketplace and remain profitable is problematic. Like any emerging business, especially in the area of technology, better companies survive and prosper; weaker ones disappear. Those who are intrigued by this part of the speaking industry and able to bring both technical and marketing skills to it may develop a successful business in cyberspace.

Directories of Speakers

Printed speaker lists have been a staple of the speaking industry from its earliest days. Today, many bureaus routinely send directories of their speakers to clients and prospects. In addition, many speakers have created speaker groups to market themselves, distributing brochures about themselves and their topics to a far bigger list than any one speaker might have developed.

A relatively recent development is the listing of speakers and consultants for journalists and talk show hosts. *The Yearbook of Experts, Authorities, and Spokespersons: An Encyclopedia of Sources,* discussed in the last chapter, is a fixture on the desk of newspaper editors, talk show producers, and broadcast hosts throughout the country. So also is the *Radio-TV Interview Report,* also previously mentioned. It bills itself as "The Magazine to Read for Guests & Show Ideas" and has generated considerable publicity for its advertisers. Each magazine has a sizable staff of persons who sell advertising space, write and edit copy, handle marketing and distribution, and perform the other standard functions of a small business.

Whether you become employed by any of the speaker marketing services—or could be successful starting some variation of speaker listings as an entrepreneur—is for you to discover. What is certain is that the speaking business is a growth industry with room for all kinds of innovation.

PUBLICISTS AND CONSULTANTS

While just about every public relations firm in the country will take on a speaker, author, or consultant—if the price is right—few are familiar with the speaking industry. On the other hand, some provide outstanding service to speakers. If you have a background that would enable you to help speakers with their publicity, you might find a role as a consultant to help speakers develop marketing plans or as a publicist who keeps speakers in the limelight. It is likely that as veteran professional speakers reduce their time on the road or retire altogether from life on the platform, many will become consultants to emerging speakers.

PUBLISHERS

This book provides an example of the output of the vast number of publishing firms that supply books on speech communication, as well as on a number of other business, personal development, sales, and other topics. As speakers discover the value of being published authors, their books are crowding the bookstore shelves, the magazine ads, and the mail order lists with titles on a wide variety of subjects. One important attraction of book publishing, from the author's point of view, is the passive income that comes in the form of royalties or the larger income that comes from the sale of self-published books. Full-time speakers especially value this income, given the unpredictability of platform fee income. Their books also gain a good deal of credibility for them.

Employment as an editor or marketer with a book publisher has provided employment for a significant number of persons with degrees in speech communication or a related field—and for others who enjoy handling materials in this field. Others have developed a business that facilitates self-publishing by speakers and trainers. The most prominent company of this kind in the speaking industry is About Books of Buena Vista, Colorado. It consults with the author throughout the process of analyzing the market, writing, editing, designing, producing, and marketing the book. Many other individuals and smaller companies work with speakers to enable them to get their books to market.

TAPE PRODUCERS

An almost indispensable element of speakers' marketing campaigns is a tape recording of their platform work—audio, video, or both. Meeting planners who do not have personal experience with a speaker or strong recommendations rely heavily on what they hear and see on tapes. Almost every town in the country of significant size boasts at least one or two small companies that tape record weddings, civic functions, and other events. These firms can supply professional quality recordings for speakers, adding opening and closing music, a voiceover by an announcer, duplication of small or large quantities, packaging, and sometimes help with distribution. Larger companies that have grown to serve a national constituency employ several people who specialize in a particular phase of the service.

The production of videotapes is considerably more complex and more expensive, but the process is much the same as the audio cassette business. It is only in the larger towns and cities that first-class video producers are available, but many smaller television stations and even cable outlets provide a videotaping service as an additional profit center, and some are of excellent quality. A few companies, like Chesney Communications of Irvine, California, and RBS Productions of Carlsbad, California, specifically address the speaker market. More companies are certain to develop as the industry grows.

The largest and best-known company that produces and distributes tapes is Nightingale-Conant of Northfield, Illinois. Its catalog has produced profit both for itself and for the speakers whose tapes are sold. Several smaller companies around the nation have developed similar operations, some marketing to a wide segment of the public and others to markets with specialized interests. The voracious appetite of the public for tapes suggests a wide-open opportunity for new tape production and distribution businesses.

INSTRUCTORS

Chapter 5 has already outlined and developed in some detail the opportunities for persons to provide presentation skills training. Thousands of people are employed to teach speech in public schools, colleges, and universities and commercial training organizations such as Dale Carnegie. Public seminar companies contribute to the speaking industry by employing many more. Additional public speaking experts, operating home-based businesses, act as coaches to business executives, politicians, and others who are developing their speaking skills. Some are experimenting with coaching via the exchange of videotapes, with responses passing between student and coach on e-mail. As long as speakers mount platforms, there will be a need for speech instructors and coaches.

There is a new development in speech instruction that has arisen to meet the need of people who wish to enter the world of paid speaking. Experienced, high-profile speakers offer to share their secrets of success with all comers, offering them books, tapes, and seminars. Several of these opportunities were discussed in Chapter 5 and more will undoubtedly arise as successful speakers offer their help to beginners.

TRAINING FRANCHISES

Many speakers who develop the training side of their businesses enter into a relationship with a company that provides ready-made training programs and materials. The Carlson Learning Company of Minneapolis is one of the largest of these companies. It features the DISC assessment system for assessing behavioral styles, well known by trainers for sales and other human relations seminars. Its Performax materials are sold to accredited distributors for their own use in conducting seminars and for resale to trainers they have recruited. These affiliates contract to attend train-the-trainer seminars and to use workbooks and software developed by the company.

A firm with a somewhat different corporate style, TTI of Scottsdale, Arizona, offers independent trainers behavioral and attitude training modules on such subjects as team building, sales, communication, and customer service. It also uses the DISC system, offering several proprietary software packages for use in training seminars. Many smaller training companies that have successfully developed and tested their own materials are offering the use of their products to speakers, generally for a percentage of the trainer's fees and sometimes just for the price of the products. There seems to be no end to the opportunity to create and sell training materials.

VENDORS

Many business organizations with ties to the speaking industry—hotels, restaurants, theaters—would thrive even if there were no speakers. Others count speakers and trainers among their most important customers—in some cases their only customers.

A glance through the pages of *Sharing Ideas* reveals a wide variety of companies that provide for the needs of people who work on the nation's platforms and in its training rooms. In just one issue, the speaker can read about many of the goods and services already described in this chapter. In addition, speakers learn they can do business with a financial services company to enable them to use Visa and other credit cards for book and tape orders; patronize a company that will help them develop a web site; utilize a dispute resolution service offered by a speaker who is also a lawyer; purchase ghostwriting services for speeches and books; contract for custom-tailored promotional and advertising services, audio recording, and duplicating equipment; adopt an integrated success system for developing a speaking business; order photo business cards with the speaker's picture in full color; and use the facilities of a yacht in southern California on which to hold seminars.

Other offerings that speakers receive in the mail from vendors or at speakers' conventions include creative teaching tools—laser and flip-chart pointers, a cartooning kit, crayons, and the like. One company offers the Speech-Lite Advanced Computerized Timer that eliminates the need for chairpersons with time cards and stopwatches, enabling the speaker to be aware of time constraints. Manufacturers of overhead projectors and notebook computers designed to create and control multimedia productions also solicit business from speakers and trainers. Many companies offer a slide imaging service that produces slides and overheads from a computer-generated file. Many speakers purchase their own portable public address system with a lapel or hand-held microphone, usually engineered as either a stand-alone system or able to connect to a meeting room's amplifier.

The goods and services described in this chapter provide powerful proof of the existence and size of the speaking industry. The business of speaking clearly does not belong simply to a lone speaker on a platform but is the means of support for a great number of people. A substantial number of them are earning their livelihoods because speakers and audiences by the thousands face each other every day.

Our nation is the stronger for the work of the people in this burgeoning industry—clearly the speakers themselves—but also those who support the words of these creative, skilled people. In a variety of ways, each person in the speaking industry is contributing to the important exchange of information and ideas indispensable to a free and just society.

Appendixes

Speaker Organizations

American Society for Training and Development
1640 King Street, PO Box 1443
Alexandria, VA 22318-2043
(703) 683-8100 Fax (703) 683-8103 www.astd.org

International Group of Agencies and Bureaus
6845 Parkdale Place, Suite A
Indianapolis, IN 46254
(317) 297-0872 Fax (317) 387-3387
75157.123@Compuserve.com www.IGAB.org

International Platform Association
PO Box 250
Winnetka, IL 60093-0250
(847) 446-4321 www.internationalplatform.com

National Association of Campus Activities
13 Harbison Way
Columbia, SC 29212-3401
(803) 732-6222 Fax (803) 749-1047
http.bbs.naca.sc.edu/index.htm

National Speakers Association
1500 S. Priest Drive
Tempe, AZ 85281
(602) 968-2552 Fax (602) 968-0911 www.nsaspeaker.org

Speech Communication Association
5105 Backlick Road, Building F
Annandale, VA 22003
(703) 750-0533 Fax (703) 914-9471 www.scassn.org

Toastmasters International
23182 Arroyo Vista
Rancho Santa Margarita
PO Box 9052
Mission Viejo, CA 92690
(714) 858-8255 Fax (714) 858-9052
TMInfo@Toastmasters.org www.toastmasters.org

Magazines/Periodicals for Speakers

Professional Speaker
(See National Speakers Association in Appendix A)
Free to NSA members; others, $49 for 10 issues

Sharing Ideas
PO Box 1120
Glendora, CA 91740
(818) 335-8069   Fax (818) 335-6127
DotWalters@AOL.com
www.walters-intl.com
$95.00 for 2 years

Storytelling Magazine
National Storytellers Association
PO Box 309
Jonesborough, TN 37659
(423) 753-2171
$40 membership, includes subscription

The Toastmaster
(See Toastmasters International in Appendix A)
sfrey@toastmasters.org
Free to members of Toastmaster clubs

Training and Development
American Society for Training and Development
Box 1443
Alexandria, VA 22313-2043
Free to ASTD members; others, $85 per year

Vital Speeches of the Day
PO Box 1247
Mount Pleasant, SC 29465
(803) 881-8733   Fax (803) 881-4007
Vitalspeeches@AWOD.com
$40.00 per year, 24 issues

Public Seminar Companies

American Management Association
135 West 50th Street
New York, NY 10020
(212) 903-7915

Career Track Seminars
PO Box 18778
Boulder, CO 80308-1778
(800) 334-6780

Dun and Bradstreet
299 Park Avenue
New York, NY 10171
(212) 593-6800

Fred Pryor Seminars
2000 Shawnee Mission Parkway
Shawnee Mission, KS 66201-1349
(913) 722-3990

Keye Productivity Center
Box 27-480
Kansas City, MO 64180
(800) 821-3919

National Seminars Group
PO Box 2949
Shawnee Mission, KS 66201-7246
(800) 258-7246

Padgett-Thompson
PO Box 8297
Overland Park, KS 66208
(800) 255-4141

SkillPath, Inc.
PO Box 2768
Mission KS 66201-2768
(800) 873-7545

Books on the Business of Speaking

Anthony, Robert. *How to Make a Fortune from Public Speaking: Put Your Money Where Your Mouth Is.* New York: Berkley, 1983.

Burgett, Gordon. *Empire-Building by Writing and Speaking: A How-To Guide for Communicators, Entrepreneurs, and Other Information Merchants.* Carpinteria, CA: Communication Unlimited, 1987. (out of print)

Burgett, Gordon, and Frank, Mike. *Speaking for Money.* Carpinteria, CA: Communication Unlimited, 1985. (out of print)

Frank, Mike. *For Professional Speakers Only.* Speakers Unlimited, Box 27225, Columbus, OH 43227, (614) 864-3703, 1995.

Gardner, Gerald. *Speech Is Golden: How to Sell Your Wit, Wisdom, Expertise, and Personal Experiences on the Local and National Lecture Circuit.* New York: St. Martin, 1992. (out of print)

Holtz, Herman. *The Business of Public Speaking.* New York: John Wiley & Sons, 1985. (out of print)

Karasik, Paul. *How to Make It Big in the Seminar Business.* New York: McGraw-Hill, 1992.

Walters, Dottie, and Walters, Lilly. *Speak and Grow Rich* (2nd edition). Englewood Cliffs, NJ: Prentice-Hall, 1997.

Sources for Finding Meeting Planners

Your local library: A reference librarian will help you.

American Society of Association Executives Membership Directory
1575 Eye Avenue NW
Washington, DC 20005
(202) 626-2723

Association Meeting Directory
1001 Connecticut Avenue NW
Suite 1005
Washington, DC 20036
(202) 296-7400

Association Meeting Planners & Conference/Convention Directors* and *Directory of Corporate Meeting Planners
(Both are also available by states)
The Salesman's Guide (Division of R. R. Bowker)
881 Broadway
New York, NY 10003
(800) 223-1797

Directory of Conventions
Successful Meetings Data Bank
633 Third Avenue
New York, NY 10017
(800) 253-6708

Encyclopedia of Associations
Gale Research, Inc.
835 Penobscot Building
Detroit, MI 48226-4094
(313) 961-2242   (800) 877-4253

National Trade and Professional Associations
Columbia Books
1212 New York Avenue, NW
Suite 330
Washington, D8
C 20005
(202) 898-0662

Some Associations That Engage Unpaid Speakers

American Association of Retired Persons
American Association of University Women
American Businesswomen's Association
American Society for Training and Development
Apartment house residents associations
Business and Professional Women
Chambers of Commerce
Church groups
Corporation retirement clubs
Exchange Clubs
General Federation of Women's Clubs
Junior Women's Clubs
Kiwanis Clubs
Libraries
Lions Clubs
Meeting Professionals International
National Association of Retired Federal Employees
Optimist Clubs
Retirement communities
Rotary Clubs
Senior citizen clubs
Sisterhoods/Brotherhoods: synagogues

Online Marketing Service Providers

The Expertise Center
(800) 648-2677
Webmaster@expertcenter.com
www.expertcenter.com

Host Hub
(503) 227-7425
staff@cmihub.com
www.cmihub.com

K. Gordon & Associates
(314) 968-9140
kgordon@kgordon.com
www.terraweb.com/K_Gordon/

NewMarket Forum
(617) 423-4373
bmcg@newmkt.com
www.newmarket-forum.com/speakers/

Public Speaker
(206) 323-7995
info@publicspeaker.com
www.publicspeaker.com

Seminar Finder
(805) 892-2386
Seminars@speaking.com
www.seminarfinder.com

Seminar Information Service, Inc.
(714) 261-9104
SemInfo@AOL.com
www.tscentral.com

Seminar TV
(619) 722-2407
success@seminartv.com
www.seminartv.com

SpeakerSearch
(301) 963-1588
Sales@SpeakerSearch.com
www.speakersearch.com

Speakers On-Line
(301) 299-6080
speakers@clark.net
www.speakers.com

Speakers Platform
(805) 892-2386
Speakers@speaking.com
www.speaking.com

Walters Speakers Services
(818) 335-8069
DotWalters@AOL.com
www.SpeakandGrowRich.com

Publicity Sources

Media Relations (Talk Radio-TV)
1550 East 78th Street
Minneapolis, MN 55423
(612) 798-7200

Radio-TV Interview Report
Bradley Communications Corp.
135 East Plumstead Ave.
PO Box 1206
Lansdowne, PA 19050-8206
(610) 259-1070 Fax (215) 284-3704

The Yearbook of Experts, Authorities, & Spokespersons
2233 Wisconsin Avenue
Washington, DC 20007
(202) 333-4904 Fax (202) 342-5411
Editor@YearbookNews.com
www.YearbookNews.com

Sample Letter to Prospects

Formal Salutation

Dear Mr./Ms. _______________:

The challenges that face your association/company do not go away easily. I do not pretend that, as a speaker, I can shoo them away. I do know that I may be able to help you and your people deal with them creatively when they come together to form an audience.

I know that people in an audience can focus intensely on a topic that they may need to hear about from someone outside their organization who speaks knowledgeably and winsomely. I know from experience that they will respond positively to what I say when I deal with _________________ _____________________ (insert your topic).

The reason I can help you is that ____________________ (insert your qualifications and experiences).

Here is what some meeting planners have said about my presentations to their organizations: _______________ (insert quotations from letters of appreciation).

I will be in touch with you by phone in the next week or so to explore the possibility of my spending some time with your people. I am confident that my ability as a dynamic speaker to deal with the challenges you face will do your organization a world of good. I trust that you will leave word to accept my call and that we can work together to make your next meeting everything you could wish for.

Cordially,

Sample Confirmation Letter

Formal Salutation

Dear Mr./Ms. ______________________________

I am pleased to confirm my appearance before the ______________________ (name of group) on ________________ (date) at ______________ (time).

My understanding is that you wish me to speak on ________________________ (topic) for a period of ___________ (minutes). (optional) I will be glad also to answer questions from the audience for a total of _____________ minutes.

(If visual aids are to be used) I shall be using as a visual aid ______________________ (name of equipment). I will bring ___________________ (items you control) and need at the site _________________ (items you wish them to provide).

We have agreed on the phone that you will provide an honorarium of $_______ (plus expenses to be billed to you separately). I would appreciate it if the honorarium check is ready for me the evening of the engagement.

I am happy to be able to work with you on this project, and I look forward eagerly to the challenge of communicating with your people.

Please call me if any questions arise between now and the meeting date.

I am committed to doing my very best for your organization.

Sincerely,

Sample Contract/ Memorandum of Agreement

Date: ________________ Agreement Number: __________

Client Name: ____

Contact: ____

Address: ____

Client Phone: ____

Speaker Name: ____

Speaker Address: ____

Speaker Phone: ____

Date of Engagement: ____

Location: ____

Time Event Begins: ____

Time Speaker Begins: ____

Length of Presentation: ______________________________________

Title of Presentation: ____

Contracted Fee: ____

Required Deposit (optional): ___________________________________

Balance (optional): ____

Special arrangements: ____

(allow space for client's provision of visual aids, transportation considerations, special menu, overnight lodging, participation in related program events, etc.)

Client and speaker agree that the above information represents the arrangements mutually agreed upon for a speaking engagement. This agreement may not be canceled by either party within a ______________ (time period) without written notice to the other.

Both copies of this agreement are to be signed by client and speaker in order for it to be valid.

________________	______	________________	______
Client	Date	Speaker	Date

Sample Speaker Evaluation Form

Speaker ____

Date ____

Organization ____

Please circle the term that describes the speaker's presentation

Excellent   Very Good   Good   Fair   Poor

The importance to you of the ideas presented

Excellent   Very Good   Good   Fair   Poor

The creativity/originality of the presentation

Excellent   Very Good   Good   Fair   Poor

The speaker's delivery—vocal and bodily factors

Excellent   Very Good   Good   Fair   Poor

If asked by another organization about this speaker, I would say:

____

____

____

____

____

Signed (Optional) _____________________________________

Sample Speaker Introduction

Today's speaker brings a wealth of knowledge and experience to our association, and a lot of insight about one of the topics that concerns all of us . . . money!

Larry Horne studied business at Michigan State (when he wasn't running up and down the basketball court as a varsity center). His grades and personality got him jobs as a financial consultant with some of the best-known firms, including Merrill Lynch and Dean Witter. He had always wanted to own his own company, and now he does, in Washington Heights. He has helped many families in this area to get their financial acts together, and we are glad to have him here today. He will talk about "What You Can Do about Today's Low Interest CD Rates."

Please join me in welcoming Larry Horne!

Sample One-Pager

Barbara L. Pagano, Ed.S.

"Fresh, compelling, eye-opening, and motivating..." Barbara is an expert in giving people tools to move beyond current levels of success. Her learning programs on leadership, credibility, gender differences and life design are distinctive.

With graduate degrees in human behavior and twenty years as a facilitator for Fortune 100 firms, Barbara is a nationally recognized speaker and executive consultant. She has given personal feedback on leadership to over 2000 men and women and is a contributing writer for business publications.

Barbara works with organizations on diversity issues with a focus on gender differences. She holds certification from the American Institute of Managing Diversity.

Barbara is a strong speaker who captivates audiences with her stories, weaves in the research and learning, warms their hearts with laughter and moves them to action. She walks her talk and focuses her energy to present fresh material with a polished, professional style.

LEARNING PROGRAMS INCLUDE:

Changing Realities*—The New Male-Female Working Partnership*—a focus on high performance partnerships in a diverse workforce, new skills, and solutions to the current gender chill in organizations.

Credibility*—The Critical Key to Success*—A riveting look at the factors in credibility, how to get it and what to do if you lose it...a program for competitive times.

Balancing Life's Priorities**—** Resulting in greater energy and commitment to work and life. Based on research on effectiveness in leadership, productive work and sustained success for professionals.

KEYNOTE PRESENTATIONS INCLUDE:

Great Landings and Roaring Seas: How to Find Success in a Changing World—An extraordinary wake-up call for long distance success in work and life...uplifting message for living in fast and changing times.

"Nothing short of superb!"

You should change the name of your organization to Executive Excellence because the quality of your presentation was nothing short of superb.

– Anita J. Jenious
Vanderbilt University
Opportunity Development Center

"Unique and practical"

Your unique and practical insights into a leader's credibility provided us with useful tools to implement change back on the job.

– Sherry E. Bormann, AVP
Federal Reserve Bank of Chicago

"Better than Covey and Naisbitt?"

People are still saying it was one of our best programs...that's great praise considering we've had people like John Naisbitt, Stephen Covey and Rosabeth Moss Kanter.

– Susan E. Gordon
CEO, Peer Learning Network

Client List Includes: AT&T, Turner Broadcasting, The Prudential, WSB-TV, Lanier Voice Products, TEC, Andersen Consulting, The Federal Reserve Bank of Chicago, Vanderbilt Medical Center, American Society for Training & Development, Southern Company, Georgia Power, Alabama Power, BellSouth, St. Joseph's Hospital, North Carolina Association of Counties, Georgia Department of Labor, Georgia Pacific, American Express, Ceridian, Corporate Travel World, BellAtlantic.

163 Holcomb Ferry Road • Roswell, Georgia 30076
Tel 770 • 640 • 6971 Fax 770 • 640 • 7406
1 • 800 • 637 • 7515 BPagano@aol.com

About Toastmasters International

If the thought of public speaking is enough to stop you dead in your tracks, it may have the same effect on your career.

While surveys report that public speaking is one of people's most dreaded fears, the fact remains that the inability to effectively deliver a clear thought in front of others can spell doom for professional progress. The person with strong communication skills has a clear advantage over tongue-tied colleagues—especially in a competitive job market.

Toastmasters International, a nonprofit educational organization, helps people conquer their pre-speech jitters. From one club started in Santa Ana, California, in 1924, the organization now has more than 170,000 members in 8,300 clubs in 62 countries.

How Does It Work?

A Toastmasters club is a "learn by doing" workshop in which men and women hone their communication and leadership skills in a friendly, supportive atmosphere. A typical club has 20 members who meet weekly or biweekly to practice public speaking techniques. Members, who pay approximately $35 in dues twice a year, learn by progressing through a series of 10 speaking assignments and being evaluated on their performance by their fellow club members. When finished with the basic speech manual, members can select from among 14 advanced programs that are geared toward specific career needs. Members also have the opportunity to develop and practice leadership skills by working in the High Performance Leadership Program.

Besides taking turns to deliver prepared speeches and evaluate those of other members, Toastmasters give impromptu talks on assigned topics, usually related to current events. They also develop listening skills, conduct meetings, learn parliamentary procedure and gain leadership experience by serving as club officers. But most importantly, they develop self-confidence from accomplishing what many once thought impossible.

The benefits of Toastmasters' proven and simple learning formula has not been lost on the thousands of corporations that sponsor in-house Toastmasters clubs as cost-efficient means of satisfying their employees' needs for communication training. Toastmasters clubs can be found in the U.S. Senate and the House of Representatives, as well as in a variety of community organizations, prisons, universities, hospitals, military bases, and churches.

How to Get Started

Most cities in North America have several Toastmasters clubs that meet at different times and locations during the week. If you are interested in forming or joining a club, call (714) 858-8255. For a listing of local clubs, call (800) WE-SPEAK, or write Toastmasters International, PO Box 9052, Mission Viejo, California 92690, USA. You can also visit our website at http://www.toastmasters.org.

As the leading organization devoted to teaching public speaking skills, we are devoted to helping you become more effective in your career and daily life.

Terrence J. McCann
Executive Director, Toastmasters International

About the National Speaker's Association

The National Speakers Association (NSA) is an international association of more than 3,700 members dedicated to advancing the art and value of experts who speak professionally. Specific purposes of NSA are:

- Defining and supporting standards of excellence in professional speaking;
- Enhancing the communication competencies and business skills of professional speakers;
- Promoting the value of professional speakers as effective sources of expertise, knowledge and insight; and
- Expanding the marketplace for professional speaking.

NSA delivers a multifaceted environment for advancing the careers of professional speakers. Virtually all of NSA's programs, meetings, publications and resources are structured around eight professional competencies. Together, they are designed to give organization and substance to the educational and professional advancement of each member. The professional competencies are: Authorship and Product Development; Managing the Business; Platform Mechanics; Presenting and Performing; Professional Awareness; Professional Relationships; Sales and Marketing; and Topic Development.

The programming for NSA's Educational Workshops, Annual Conventions and single-focus Learning Labs are based on these competencies. While a minimum number of paid presentations must be documented to qualify a speaker for membership in NSA, nonmembers are welcome to attend chapter and national meetings and can subscribe to *Professional Speaker* magazine.

For more information, contact the National Speakers Association, 1500 S. Priest Drive, Tempe, Arizona 85281; Phone: 602-968-2552; Fax: 602-968-0911; E-mail: nsamain@aol.com; Web Site: http://www.nsaspeaker.org.